CURRENT TRENDS IN PSYCHOLOGY SERIES

UNIVERSITY OF PITTSBURGH PRESS

CURRENT TRENDS IN PSYCHOLOGY $4.00

Psychology As a Profession, Wayne Dennis; *Experimental Psychology,* B. F. Skinner; *Child Psychology,* Robert R. Sears; *Clinical Psychology,* E. Lowell Kelly; *Psychotherapy,* Carl Rogers; *Personnel Psychology,* John C. Flanagan; *Human Engineering,* Clifford T. Morgan; *The Sample Interview Survey,* Rensis Likert.

CURRENT TRENDS IN SOCIAL PSYCHOLOGY $4.00

The New Social Psychology, Wayne Dennis; *A Program of Experimentation on Group Functioning and Group Productivity,* Ronald Lippitt; *Cultural Diversity and World Peace,* K. T. Behanan; *An Approach to Social Perception,* Jerome S. Bruner and Leo Postman; *Experimental Sociometry and the Experimental Method in Science,* J. L. Moreno; *The Social Psychology of Housing,* Robert K. Merton; *Communication Research and the Social Psychologist,* Paul F. Lazarsfeld; *Psychological Approaches to the Prevention of War,* James G. Miller.

CURRENT TRENDS IN INDUSTRIAL PSYCHOLOGY $4.00

The Background of Industrial Psychology, Wayne Dennis; *Organization Structure,* Carroll L. Shartle; *Job Requirements,* John C. Flanagan; *Personnel Selection,* Orlo L. Crissey; *Training in Industry,* William McGehee; *Employee-Management Relations,* Brent Baxter; *Morale and Motivation in Industry,* Daniel Katz; *Industrial Psychology and the Community,* Harold C. Taylor.

CURRENT TRENDS IN THE RELATION OF PSYCHOLOGY TO MEDICINE $4.00

Interrelations of Psychology and Medicine, Wayne Dennis; *Psychology and Public Health,* Robert H. Felix, M. D.; *Psychology in Medical Education,* Carlyle Jacobsen; *Experimental Psychopathology,* Robert A. Patton; *Psychology in Neurological Research,* Y. D. Koskoff, M. D.; *Psychology in Relation to Psychiatry,* Paul E. Huston, M. D.; *Psychology and Gerontology,* Nathan W. Shock; *The Relation Between Medicine and Psychology in England,* Hans J. Eysenck.

CURRENT TRENDS IN PSYCHOLOGICAL THEORY $4.00

Developmental Theories, Wayne Dennis; *Theories of Personality,* Robert Leeper; *Learning Theories,* Harry F. Harlow; *Theories of Perception,* James J. Gibson; *Cognition and Motivation in Psychological Theory,* David Krech; *Theories of Psychotherapy,* David McK. Rioch, M.D.; *Brain and Behavior,* W. S. McCulloch, M.D.; *Principles and Problems of Theory Construction in Psychology,* Herbert Feigl.

Current Trends in Psychology in the World Emergency — $4.00

Psychology in the World Emergency, John C. Flanagan; *Research in Military Leadership,* Fillmore H. Sanford; *Problems in the Administration and Utilization of Contract Research,* John W. Macmillan; *The Uses and Limitations of Mathematical Models, Game Theory, and Systems Analysis in Planning and Problem Solution,* John L. Kennedy; *Military Requirements for the Systematic Study of Psychological Variables,* Arthur W. Melton; *Psychological Warfare, Strategic Intelligence, and Overseas Research in the World Emergency,* Frederick W. Williams; *Matching Personnel and Jobs,* Donald E. Baier; *Organization and Opportunities in Service Programs of Psychological Research,* Glen Finch.

Current Trends in Information Theory — $4.00

Mathematical Aspects of Information Theory, Brockway McMillan; *Information Theory and the Discrimination of Sequences in Stimulus Events,* David A. Grant; *The Influence of Response Coding on Performance in Motor Tasks,* Paul M. Fitts; *Some Perceptual Problems from the Point of View of Information Theory,* Frederick C. Frick; *Information in the Head,* Warren S. McCulloch; *Information Theory and the Study of Speech,* George A. Miller; *Information Theory and Clinical Medicine (Psychiatry),* Henry W. Brosin.

Current Trends in Psychology and the Behavioral Sciences — $4.00

Psychology and Behavioral Science, John T. Wilson; *Some Potential Contributions of Anthropology to Psychology,* Clellan S. Ford; *The Science of Learning and the Art of Teaching,* B. F. Skinner; *Reduction,* Gustav Bergmann; *The Individual from Conception to Conceptualization,* Frank A. Beach; *Toward a Science of Neuropsychology (Method and Data),* Karl Pribram.

Current Trends in the Description and Analysis of Behavior — $4.00

Descriptive Variables for the Study of Task-oriented Groups, Robert Glaser; *A Biometric Model for Psychopathology,* Joseph Zubin; *Psychology and Perception,* Donald B. Lindsley; *On the Use of Drugs in the Analysis of Complex Human Behavior with Emphasis on the Study of Mood,* Vincent Nowlis; *The Mediation Hypothesis in the Analysis and Description of Behavior,* Charles N. Cofer; *Interaction Between Methods and Models in Social Psychology,* Harold Guetzkow; *Process and Content in Psycholinguistics,* John B. Carroll; *Scientific Methodology in the Area of Psychotherapy,* Roy M. Hamlin; *Guilt, Shame, and Other Reactive Motives,* Thomas M. French.

CURRENT TRENDS IN THE DESCRIPTION AND ANALYSIS OF BEHAVIOR

Nine lectures

under the auspices of

the Department of Psychology in The College

of the University of Pittsburgh

delivered during March 11 and 12, 1955

and March 8 and 9, 1956

in the Stephen Foster Memorial Auditorium

CURRENT TRENDS IN THE DESCRIPTION AND ANALYSIS OF BEHAVIOR

ROBERT GLASER
JOSEPH ZUBIN
DONALD B. LINDSLEY
VINCENT NOWLIS
CHARLES N. COFER
HAROLD GUETZKOW
JOHN B. CARROLL
ROY M. HAMLIN
THOMAS M. FRENCH

1958
UNIVERSITY OF PITTSBURGH PRESS

LIBRARY OF CONGRESS CATALOG CARD NUMBER: 58-7146

PRINTED IN U.S.A. BY DAVIS & WARDE, INC., PITTSBURGH, PA.

CURRENT TRENDS IN THE DESCRIPTION AND ANALYSIS OF BEHAVIOR

PREFACE

EACH year since 1947 the University of Pittsburgh has sponsored a conference dealing with current advances and probable future developments in an active area of psychology.

This year the departmental committee was interested in the general problem of measurement since there is the continuous need for the development of methods to quantify the stubborn and elusive phenomena of behavior. The title selected was "The Description and Analysis of Behavior." Most of the papers in the present volume deal with this topic although the invited speakers were free to suggest their individual titles.

Three additional contributions by Roy Hamlin, Harold Guetzkow, and John Carroll were presented at the previous conference and are included here.

These papers are presented without the discussion which they elicited from the audience and from the other speakers. It is our hope, however, that they reflect a stimulating and valuable experience for all who attended the conference.

ROBERT A. PATTON

DESCRIPTIVE VARIABLES FOR THE STUDY OF TASK-ORIENTED GROUPS

ROBERT GLASER

The work reported here was performed as a portion of a research project sponsored by the Psychological Sciences Division of the Office of Naval Research. I am indebted to my colleague, Dr. Murray Glanzer, who worked with me in developing the notions presented in this paper. Mr. Alan W. Morten, Jr., contributed substantially in suggesting and working out many important details.

A CURRENT trend in social psychology and in the application of psychological research to military problems has been the study of working groups, or as they may be called, teams or crews. Research programs are being undertaken to study the behavior of these kinds of groups and, more practically, to develop methods for team training and the improvement of team operations.[8] A basic problem in this work is the development of a descriptive system or set of terms by which the operation and structure of a team can be described. This involves the identification of the relevant variables and the development of methods for their measurement. Once this is accomplished, the relationship of these variables to group behavior can then be studied. I should like to report at this time some initial work in this direction, that is, in the development of a set of terms or dimensions for the description of certain collections of individuals. Our concern has been with the development of descriptive procedures, definitions, and measurement procedures that can be used to describe the differences between working groups. This paper consists essentially of three parts: (1) a brief account of the past work that has influenced our thinking, (2) an overview of our own work, and (3) some suggested directions for further research.

The kinds of groups with which we are concerned have certain special characteristics. They are, as social psychologists say, formal groups as contrasted with informal groups. Most studies of group behavior have been concerned with informal groups; these are collections of individuals who must decide upon their goals, and upon the tasks and procedures to achieve these goals. Formal groups, on the other hand, have a relatively clear-cut mission, their procedures are pretty much standardized, and status and leadership hierarchies are established.

Another distinction that can be made in considering the study of groups is a distinction between "social process variables" and "task variables." "Social process variables" refer to behavior that is primarily associated with attitudes, morale, group cohesion, group conformity, and so forth. "Task variables" refer to behavior that is directly required for performance of the work the group has to accomplish.

The distinctions made between formal and informal groups and between social-process and task variables help define the specific subject matter which is our concern, that is, the task behavior of formal groups. With respect to this subject matter, I should like to report the results of some observation and some thinking on the kinds of variables which might be used to describe the structure and functioning of these groups of individuals.

As reported in the literature, the bulk of the research on group behavior has been concerned with social-process variables in informal groups and to a lesser extent in formal groups. The study of task variables has received less emphasis. Social behavior and task-related behaviors together comprise the related classes of events which we call group performance. A comprehensive model of group behavior should consider both of these classes. The emphasis of the research done to date exposes the social psychologists to the danger of producing models of group performance based primarily on the social-process class of events.

Recently, studies of the task-related behavior of individuals and the resulting group behavior have been increasing, and work in a number of areas has been available to facilitate our thinking. Let me briefly consider four major influences, namely, (1) sociometry, (2) the study of communication networks, (3) the use of graph theory, and (4) what I shall call activity category analysis.

The work in sociometry has been primarily concerned with the pattern or structure of choice and rejection within a group. In this context there has been a considerable development of techniques for the description of groups in terms of these relationships between members. Originally, sociometric procedures were primarily graphical; more recently sociometric data have been cast into the form of n-by-n matrices and the operations of matrix algebra utilized. The work in sociometry has been concerned to a great extent with indexes of group structure such as group expansiveness, group interaction, dominance relationships, and the identification of subgroups. While sociometry has not been concerned with task variables, its techniques, devised for the relationships of choice and rejection, appear to be applicable to analysis of the relationships between the inputs and outputs resulting from the performance of task activities.

While sociometric studies have been concerned with describing group structure, the work done on communication networks following from the work of Bavelas[3, 4] has consisted of imposing certain communication networks upon small task-oriented groups in the laboratory. The relationship between different communication patterns and certain aspects of group social and task behavior is then studied. With respect to the description of group communication patterns, Bavelas employs the procedure of counting the communication linkages between individuals. On this basis he suggests indexes of the "dispersion" of communication patterns and the "relative centrality" of individual positions in a pattern. Centrality refers to the extent to which a position is connected by a minimum number of communication links to other members in the group. Leavitt[12] working with Bavelas considers such descriptive variables of group communication structure as the "relative peripherality" of different positions in a group. With respect to the properties of entire group patterns, he mentions "pattern flexibility," which refers to the extent to which a group uses certain linkage combinations out of all communication channels available to them to solve a problem. He also refers to "operational flexibility," which describes the particular ways in which communication between group members can occur within a specific combination of channel linkages.

In a working paper, Christie, Luce, and Macy[5] describe additional aspects of communication. They derive indexes which they label "input density" and "input potential." These indexes deal essentially with the mean number of input stimuli or messages per act, and the mean number of inputs per unit time. In their work these investigators consider information theory and similar probability models in interpreting their findings on the behavior of task-oriented groups.

Gilchrist, Shaw, and Walker[7] have employed the term "saturation" to refer to the interaction of the centrality of a position and its demands in terms of a required level of output message units. Shaw[13] utilizes a measure of the degree of "independence" with which an individual may function in a task-oriented group. This measure takes into account the number of communication channels available to the individual, the number of channels available to the group, and the number of individuals for which a given position serves as a relayer of information. I should note here that as a result of my concern in this paper with descriptive measures, I have considered only these aspects in the studies mentioned and obviously have not attempted to report their research findings.

Akin to the work in sociometry and communication networks is a monograph by Harary and Norman[10] which considers the use of the definitions and concepts of the theory of graphs as a mathematical model for the study of the structure of the communication network in a group. Graph theory considers a finite collection of points and the set of lines joining pairs of these points. As applied to groups, the points correspond to individuals and the lines to communication links. In their monograph, the authors present many of the classical definitions in graph theory, following the work of Kónig,[11] together with some applications to the subject matter of psychology. The authors hope to encourage the use of a uniform language using graph theory terms. This work is recent and its use has not as yet been extensive.

The work I have mentioned so far concentrates upon communication linkages. Another relatively large group of studies have been concerned with the description of group functioning in terms of a general set of categories or a category system by which the activities of the group members, with respect to the group task, can be described. For particular kinds of groups and for particular kinds of problem-solving tasks, the frequency and pattern of the occurrence of these categories over time is recorded. The basic work employing this procedure is the work of Bales.[1] Bales's categories are designed for discussion groups. Christie, Luce and Macy,[5] and Forgays and Roby[6] suggest categories more pertinent to formal task-oriented groups.

Having described our interests and influences, let me proceed to our approach. Description of the operation of formal task-oriented groups can be made in terms of the group members with respect to three classes of events, namely, behavioral acts, sequence or time flow, and communication flow. The basic unit of description is called an act. An act consists of the following elements: input, process, and output. Input consists of the signals or stimuli that elicit certain behavior; process is the behavior carried out by the group member; and output consists of the signals or stimuli resulting from the process carried out. Thus, in a gunnery team, if a member sees a target, determines its range and bearing, and shouts out his result, input, process, and output respectively, are: the radar scope signals, the determination of range and bearing, and the calling out of range and bearing. For certain descriptive purposes these acts are classified into a number of categories, namely, observing, relaying, manipulating, computing, and deciding.

Sequence or time flow is introduced into a description of team operation by ordering the acts of the members according to the time periods and sequence in which they occur.

Communication flow between group members, that is, intra-team communication links, can be described in graphical form by directional arrows or in terms of matrix entries. Extra-team communication links, that is, inputs and outputs to and from the environment defined as external to the group, are also indicated in this way. The word "communication" is broadly used here and refers to all interaction between team members that is necessary for accomplishing the task. Communication consists of the response outputs of an individual that serve as input stimuli for other individuals. These can consist of such things as verbal commands, hand signals, control manipulations, etc.

These three aspects of group functioning, acts, sequence, and communication flow, can be combined into a working diagram which schematically looks thus:

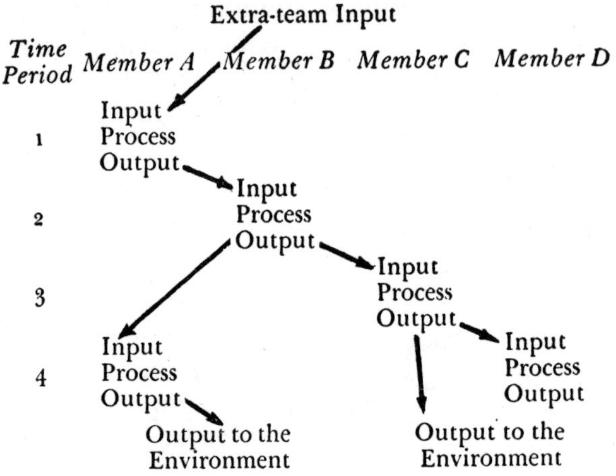

Notice in this diagram that all members do not send to or receive information from the environment; and that Member D stores his output.

A matrix of communication flow between members would look something like this:

	Recipient					
Sender	*A*	*B*	*C*	*D*	E*	*Total*
A	0	3			1	4
B		0	1		3	4
C	2		0	1		3
D		1	1	0	1	3
E*	3				0	3
Total	5	4	2	1	5	17

E* = Environment

This matrix shows that Member A sends three messages to Member B and one message to the environment. Member B sends one message to Member C and three messages to the environment. As recipient, A receives two messages from C and three from the environment; B receives three messages from A and one message from D.

With the basic data I have just described obtained for a group, a number of descriptive variables or dimensions of group structure and group functioning can be computed. Omitting computational details, I should now like to present thirteen descriptive variables which we have been considering for use in the study of task-oriented groups. Measures of many of these variables have been computed for a wide variety of military teams in a project sponsored by the Office of Naval Research.[9] These dimensions can be categorized into three somewhat overlapping classes: (1) communication variables, those concerned primarily with link structure and the properties of the communication between individuals or between individuals and the environment; (2) time sequence variables, those concerned with the relationship of acts in the course of time; and (3) process variables, those concerned with the classes of acts carried out during group functioning. The thirteen variables which I shall describe are:

Communication Variables

(Intra-Group Communication)

1. Link Frequency
2. Communication Frequency
3. Communication Significance

4. Input Magnitude

Communication Variables

(Extra-Group Communication)

5. Output Irrevocability
6. Intra-team Dependence
7. Saturation

Time Sequence Variables

8. Sequence Predictability
9. Concurrent Activity
10. Anticipatory Cuing
11. Urgency

Process Variables

12. Process Differentiation
13. Process Flow

I shall consider now variables primarily concerned with communication; the first of these is *Link Frequency*. This refers to the number of links over which the members of a group communicate. It is defined as the total number of links over which one or more messages are sent. It can be considered as a measure of the "complexity" of the group's communication structure. In terms of link frequency we can measure the extent to which each individual can communicate with other individuals. In addition, the number of input and output links associated with a position can indicate the "load" on a group member in the sense that he must attend to and contribute to information from a particular number of channels.

A second descriptive variable is *Communication Frequency*. Link frequency just described is concerned only with the presence or absence of links. Communication frequency refers to the extent to which these links are used. This can be considered to be a measure of the general "activeness" of the interaction between group members. Frequently used links and links which are sole sources of information take on special importance for certain purposes.

Communication Significance. Certain members of a group act as central points for receiving and transmitting messages. Individuals at such points can process and integrate a large number of messages or can be the primary connection between subgroups. Such communication points can be vulnerable parts of a group structure in the face of disrupting influences. Graph theory notions talk of such points in terms of "bridges" and "articulation points" connecting subgraphs.

Input Magnitude. This is concerned with the complexity of the input stimuli that are received by group members. It describes the extent to which the group members handle simultaneous input stimuli. The complexity or simplicity of certain team tasks is, in part, a function of the number of different, conflicting, or corroboratory inputs that must be responded to or taken into account before an act is performed. The functioning of one group may require that 75 per cent of the inputs to members consist of one message; analysis of another group may show that 50 per cent of its inputs consist of three or more simultaneous messages.

The first four variables mentioned, link frequency, communication frequency, communication significance, and input magnitude, have been concerned primarily with communication between group members. Although input magnitude, for instance, can describe *both* intra-team stimuli and extra-team inputs from the environment. The next three variables consider relationships primarily between the group and extra-team sources. The first of these is *Output Irrevocability*. This describes the extent to which outputs occur in the course of group functioning which, once relayed, leave the control of the group and have little possibility of being corrected or changed. In the operation of military groups, examples of this are the command to fire a gun or to catapult a plane.

Intra-team Dependence. This descriptive variable is concerned with the extent to which group input stimuli are generated by group members in contrast to extra-team sources. To the extent that a group is self-contained in this sense, more internal control of its functioning is possible.

Saturation. This refers to the extent to which a group is likely to receive inputs from external sources at a greater rate than it can adequately respond to. This may be a function of the number of discrete messages or the rate at which these inputs are received. Stimulus overloading of this sort results in outputs that are incorrect, delayed, or not forthcoming. Certain groups may be very susceptible to quick saturation; other groups, because of their communication structure or the kind of information they process, may be more resistant to breakdown resulting from a high rate of external inputs. A measure of the effects of this variable is best obtained under conditions where input rate can be systematically varied.

This completes the listing of some group dimensions

that are primarily concerned with describing communication structure between individuals in a group and between these individuals and the external environment. In our work with these variables we have found that our measures need to be revised or elaborated to take account of the following:

First, a communication link analysis should be devised to handle the amount of information contributed by each link. As a descriptive variable, input magnitude, for example, should be refined by taking into account the informational relationships of simultaneous inputs. If most of the simultaneous inputs which group members receive are corroboratory, i.e., they check each other, group performance will probably be more stable and reliable. On the other hand, if performance depends upon single inputs or upon simultaneous inputs which need to be integrated, performance may be less reliable.

Secondly, if measures like these are to be used to evaluate differences between teams, it would be desirable to obtain estimates of their fluctuation or variance for a large sample of different kinds of groups. This work would also be applicable to some of the additional measures I shall mention.

I shall turn now to some descriptive variables which involve time sequence relationships in group functioning. The first of these is *Sequence Predictability.* This is concerned with the extent to which the acts that occur over the course of group functioning can be predicted on the basis of preceding acts. In a group that accomplishes a task by just relaying signals from member to member, the acts performed by all members can be predicted readily once the initial act is given. On the other hand, in another kind of group, the acts performed by members and the sequence of these acts may vary frequently on the basis of intervening contingencies which arise. In this latter kind of group the acts of group members are less predictable. Two major influences affect sequence predictability, namely, decisions made by group members and inputs received from sources outside the group. Either of these can change the course of team functioning. When a decision or external input intervenes, a given act can result in alternative outputs; this, of course, makes the occurrence of future acts less predictable. A measure of the sequence predictability of a group is defined in terms of the number of highly predictable acts between these intervening factors. This reflects the degree to which the acts in a group can be predicted from the initial input in the sequence. It might be mentioned here that one of the aims underlying the setting up and training of working groups might be to increase sequence predictability, assuming that high predictability means less uncertainty and greater automaticity. This should be accompanied by the possibility of fewer errors of performance.

Another descriptive variable is *Concurrent Activity*. This refers to the extent to which the individuals in a group are all acting at the same time. During periods of high concurrent activity the group may be most susceptible to disruption by outside stresses. The possibilities of error may be high because individuals are less able to observe and monitor each other's performance. The degree of concurrent activity in a group is defined as the average number of individuals acting during the same time period; variability of concurrent activity is defined as the extent to which concurrent activity varies during the course of group functioning. In military teams we have plotted the occurrence of peak periods of concurrent activity in order to recommend that arrangements for a maximum number of monitoring and supervisory personnel be made at these times.

Anticipatory Cuing. When the acts performed by group members occur in a set sequence, a member receives cues to act not only from an immediately preceding input but from the observation of events which occur prior to this input, if such observation is possible. These observations can "warn" group members that their turn to respond in a certain way will occur at a given time. The degree of anticipatory cuing in a group is defined in terms of the number of observable events prior to input for the acts performed by team members.

Urgency. This is a descriptive variable directly concerned with the time requirements under which the functioning of a group takes place. It is defined in terms of the difference between the time taken to perform an act and the amount of time available to perform it.

Let me consider, now, process variables which are concerned with the classes of acts carried out during group functioning. As I have indicated previously, in the basic description of group operation we have classified acts in terms of the following set of categories: observing, relaying, manipulating, computing, and deciding. With respect to these categories we have defined a descriptive variable called *Process Differentiation*. This refers to the extent to which the acts performed by group members fall into different process categories and the extent to which a group is, for example, primarily an observing type of team or a decision-making team. In this connection we have also employed the variable *Process Flow* to describe the frequency with which the categories occur and change during the time of group functioning. Process flow is indicated graphically by recording time periods on a horizontal axis and recording the frequency of each category for each time period on a vertical axis. This can show the phases through which a group goes in the course of accomplishing a task. Figure 1 and Figure 2 illustrate this for two different Navy teams. Note in these figures, as examples, that manipulating processes occur only near the beginning of team activity for Team A and occur quite frequently in the course of operations for Team B. Deciding processes occur in the middle of operations for Team B and more frequently throughout operations for Team A. A number of previous studies[2, 6] have postulated regular phases through which group functioning passes. Our work with process flow in military groups, using the above categories of activities, has shown little relationship between the categories and time. It has seemed that team phases are dependent upon the specific tasks performed.

This concludes the listing of the descriptive variables we have considered for the study of task-oriented groups. They are, at best, first approximations, but I

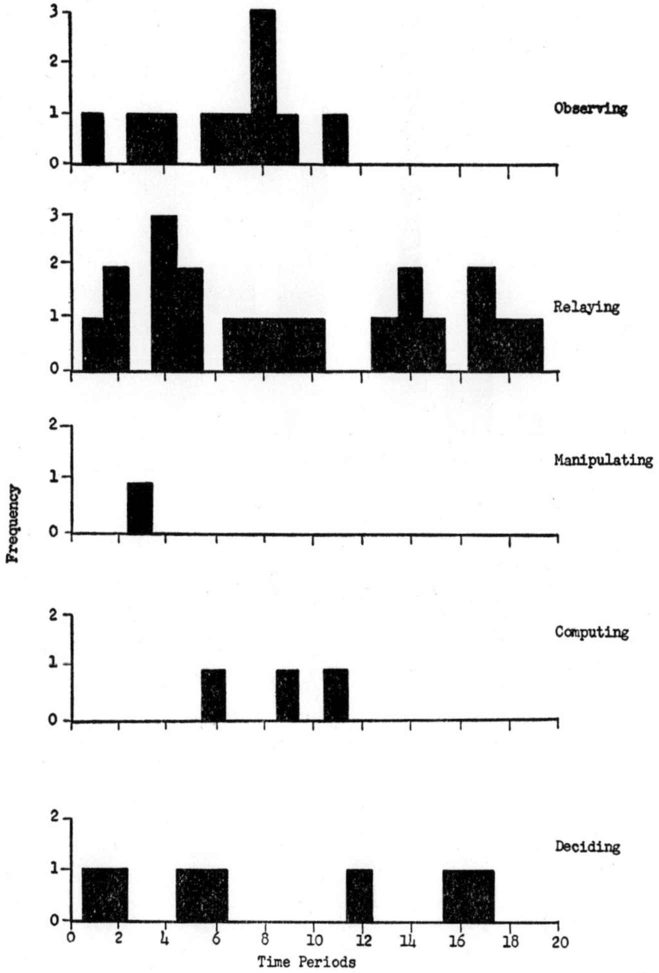

FIGURE 1. Process Flow—Team A

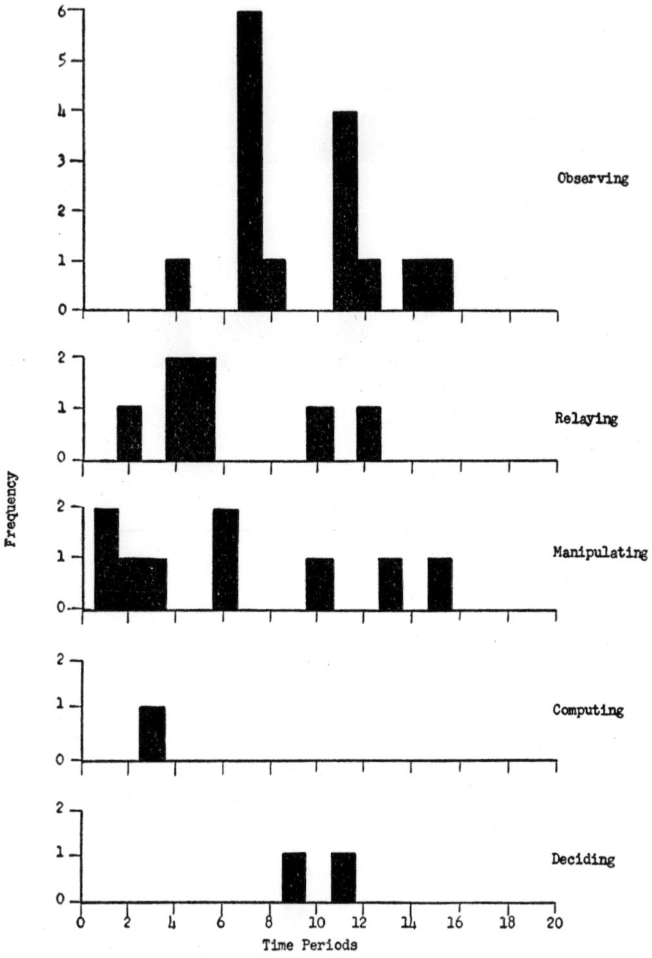

FIGURE 2. Process Flow—Team B

hope that perhaps they are provocative enough to stimulate others to do better. It seems to me that there are three major directions that further work along these lines can be expected to follow. These are: the development of refined measurement procedures, the development of testable hypotheses, and generalization of the findings.

First, *Measurement Procedures.* The specific procedures by which indexes of the descriptive variables are computed need to be refined by the application of some formal schema. Such a schema might employ the notions of graph theory; it might assign informational values to inputs and outputs; it might work with the probabilities of occurrence of alternative inputs and outputs; and it might handle categorical process data in a quantified manner.

Second, *Testable Hypotheses.* Employing available measures of team structure and functioning, a detailed model needs to be developed on the basis of which hypotheses of group behavior can be derived. These hypotheses would be stated in operational terms so that descriptive variables, such as I have listed, could be systematically varied and the resultant change in group behavior determined.

Third, *Generalization.* Since our notions developed primarily from the observation of military teams, it would seem desirable to extend the scope of the definitions presented here by considering a wider variety of groups. However, it might be advisable to ask our dimensions to first prove their worth with respect to the kinds of groups on which they were originally formulated.

In conclusion, the concern in all this is, of course, to obtain enough knowledge about the functional relationships involved, so that we can predict and manipulate group behavior. Our initial preoccupation with the development of some descriptive procedures and definitions, based upon the study of operating groups, should help bring us into range so that we will not fall too short of this mark.

REFERENCES

1. Bales, R. F. *Interaction Process Analysis: A Method for the Study of Small Groups.* Cambridge, Mass.: Addison-Welsey Press, 1951.
2. Bales, R. F., and Strodtbeck, F. L. Phases in group problem solving. *J. Abnorm. Soc. Psychol.,* 1951, 46: 485-95.
3. Bavelas, A. A mathematical model for group structures. *Appl. Anthrop.,* 1948, 7: 16-30.
4. ———. Communication patterns in task-oriented groups. *J. Acoust. Soc. Amer.,* 1950, 22: 725-30.
5. Christie, L. S., Luce, R. D., and Macy, J., Jr. *Communication and Learning in Task-oriented Groups.* MIT Research Laboratory of Electronics, U. S. Air Force Project Rand. Santa Monica: The Rand Corp., 1953.
6. Forgays, D. G., and Roby, T. B. *A Problem-solving Model for Analysis of Communication in B-29 Crews.* Research Bulletin 53-30, Human Resources Research Center. San Antonio: Lackland Air Force Base, 1953.
7. Gilchrist, J. C., Shaw, M. E., and Walker, L. C. Some effects of unequal distribution of information in a wheel group structure. *J. Abnorm. Soc. Psychol.,* 1954, 49: 554-56.
8. Glanzer, M. A., and Glaser, R. *A Review of Team Training Problems.* Office of Naval Research Technical Report. Pittsburgh: American Institute for Research, September, 1955.
9. Glaser, R., Glanzer, M. A., and Morten, A. W., Jr. *A Study of Some Dimensions of Team Performance.* Office of Naval Research Technical Report. Pittsburgh: American Institute for Research, September, 1955.

10. Harary, F., and Norman, R. Z. *Graph Theory as a Mathematical Model in Social Science.* Ann Arbor: University of Michigan, Institute for Social Research, 1953.

11. Kónig, D. *Theorie der Endlichen und Unendlichen Graphen.* (Reprinted New York: Chelsea Publishing Co., 1950.) Leipzig, 1936.

12. Leavitt, H. J. Some effects of certain communication patterns on group performance. *J. Abnorm. Soc. Psychol.,* 1951, 46: 38-50.

13. Shaw, M. E. Group structure and the behavior of individuals in small groups. *J. Psychol.,* 1954, 38: 139-49.

A BIOMETRIC MODEL FOR PSYCHOPATHOLOGY

JOSEPH ZUBIN

The author is grateful to his colleague, Dr. Eugene I. Burdock, associate research scientist (biometrics), New York State Department Mental Hygiene, for his help in preparing this paper which was facilitated in part by a research grant, M-586 (C) Psychological Prognosis in Early and Chronic Schizophrenic Patients, from the National Institute of Mental Health, of the National Institutes of Health, Public Health Service.

INTRODUCTION

PSYCHOPATHOLOGY has been defined in a variety of ways, but the common denominator underlying these definitions has not yet been discovered. Most people express great surprise when informed that there are certain regularities in the behavior of the mentally ill. The bizarre and impulsive activities often exhibited by psychotics, the sudden onset of the illness and its often equally sudden disappearance or swift progress to a chronic state, give the impression that psychopathology is lawless. Psychopathologists, however, have made a vast number of observations which, upon analysis, demonstrate a regularity and even predictability for certain types of abnormal behavior. Unfortunately most of these observations are highly subjective and based on self-referred evaluations of the observer rather than on objective criteria.

It is our purpose today to suggest a framework, a scientific model if you will, for systematizing some of the regularities which have already been noted. For the facts in this field are multiplying at such a rapid rate that they may become a hazard rather than a help for scientific advance unless some generalizations are harvested. A scientific model capitalizes on the implications of the regularities and invariances already discovered and provides a direction for future experiments.

Science progresses through two complementary processes: (1) observation and (2) schematization, which interact in the production and continual improvement of scientific models.* The scientific model thus serves a double purpose: first, it is a device for arranging observations into an ordered system for easy comprehension, and second, it is a guide or logical mechanism for reaching out into the unknown. Scientific models usually display three major constituents: (1) definitions, (2) assumptions, and (3) propositions. The definitions prescribe procedures which show how the contents of observations are to be abstracted to provide elements for the model. In physics, for example, velocity and acceleration were terms which had acquired conventional definitions. Thus Newton could use them in building his gravitational model of the universe. In psychology, sensation and perception might become such terms if their referents could be restricted by convention to recognized sets of elementary observations. The assumptions used in a model are elementary statements about the terms which have

*For a more definitive discussion of models see references 2, 20, and 22.

been defined. An example is Newton's assumption that the mass of an object can be regarded as concentrated at its center of gravity or that velocity at a point in space can be regarded as the limit of the velocities associated with the vanishingly small regions in the neighborhood of the point. A corresponding psychological assumption is that a sensation is a modality-specific abstract which can be viewed as a limiting instance of perceptual experience.

By systematic application of the assumptions to the elementary terms in accordance with the rules of logic a set of propositions may be evolved. The definitions, in turn, provide the connecting link which permits the propositions to be translated into statements about the real world. Such statements derived from an abstract model represent the predictions or hypotheses which the model offers for experimental verification.

The power of an abstract model is its capacity to generate testable hypotheses, i.e. hypotheses which can be verified by observation or experiment. Since no model includes all the minutiae of the real world, a certain looseness of fit is to be expected between an abstract proposition and the corroborative observations. Statistical theory provides the criteria for determining whether the observed discrepancies are too large for the retention of a hypothesis. A hypothesis that has survived an experimental test is not thereby affirmed; rather its rejection is suspended. It remains on sufferance. A more sensitive test may subsequently lead to its demise or an alternative hypothesis may secure more substantial experimental support, thereby leading to revision of the underlying model or, in the extreme case, to its replacement by a better-fitting model. Thus, the relativity model proposed by Einstein has replaced the gravitational model proposed earlier by Newton because the data obtained in later and more delicate experiments fitted Einstein's model more closely.*

What has been the history of model-making in psychopathology? Psychopathology is in the same position today that astronomy was before Newton. There is a considerable amount of data of all degrees of reliability. There are the models provided by Kraepelin, Freud, Meyer, and their followers. But the logical approach of theory construction and the observational approach do not mesh. Wittgenstein[18] has pointed out: "The confusion and barrenness of psychology is not to be explained by calling it a 'young science'; its state is not comparable with that of physics, for instance, in its beginnings, (rather with that of certain branches of mathematics–set theory). For in psychology there are experimental methods and conceptual confusion (as in the other case conceptual confusion and methods of proof). The existence of experimental methods makes us think we have the means of solving the problems which trouble us; though problems and methods pass one another by." The current models in psychopathology do not provide sufficiently rigid frameworks for testing their implications through direct observa-

*An eclipse expedition to Sumatra measured the deviation of stellar light under the influence of the sun's gravitational field. According to Einstein's Theory, the relation between distance from the sun and deviation should be a hyperbola. Although the stars showed a large dispersion, when the curve was determined by the method of least squares a quantitative test of the theory was obtained.[4]

tion, and the observations themselves do not provide any systematic cohesion from which theoretical models can be constructed, except in limited areas.

While Newton was faced with the task of integrating the observational data of Tycho Brahe with the geocentric hypothesis of Ptolemy and the heliocentric hypothesis of Kepler and Copernicus, abnormal psychology today has to integrate the observations of men like Kraepelin with the ego-centered hypotheses of Freud and the socio-centered concepts of Sullivan, not to mention the electrophysiological, biochemical, and surgical approaches of modern neuro-physiology and neuropsychology. Newton had to dispose of the anthropomorphic characteristics with which Aristotle had invested earth, water, air, and fire, while modern psychopathologists are faced with a similar problem in dealing with will, motivation, learning, etc. Just what disposition will be made of these constructs, whether they are necessary for the understanding of abnormal behavior, is still a moot question. Abnormal psychology is waiting for its Newton to provide new integrating concepts.

What have been the successful models in psychopathology? Despite our tendency to regard general paresis and pellagra with psychosis, for example, as no longer important in the spectrum of mental diseases, it was but yesterday that they were regarded with the same confusion that now meets the eye in schizophrenia. It is interesting to take a glimpse at the history of these diseases. General paresis was a scourge of mankind for centuries and many models of the mechanism of this disease were constructed consciously or unconsciously in an attempt to explain it. Since nightworkers in restaurants and theaters were more prone to develop general paresis, the "night air" was regarded as a culprit and closing the windows at night was recommended as a preventive. Because actors and artists seemed more susceptible, the emotional experiences that these artists underwent nightly were blamed. Krafft-Ebing[11] reports that one of his students noted that 60 per cent of the patients suffering from general paresis in his clinic had a definite history of infection with syphilis and an additional 20 per cent gave evidence of probable infection. The student, according to the story, concluded that syphilis was the underlying cause. It followed that even those general paretics who gave no history of syphilis must have had the disease and that consequently all paretics should be immune against reinfection. To test his hypothesis he proposed to inject syphilitic matter into nine moribund general paretics who gave no history of previous infection with syphilis. Krafft-Ebing reports that he was at first horrified at the suggestion, but finally consented to the experiment. All the subjects responded to the vaccination with apparent immunity. Thus the infectious disease model was introduced as applicable to general paresis. This evidence was not finally accepted until Moore and Noguchi isolated the spirochete from the brains of paretic patients. In pellagra, similarly, a great variety of approaches was tried until finally the model of dietary deficiency was suggested and found to be applicable. Currently, certain genetic and biochemical causes are being suggested for schizophrenia, but determination of their relevance awaits suitable methods for testing the hypotheses to be derived from these models. (One hypothesis emanating from the adrenochrome model for schizophrenia is that there should be fewer blonds among schizophrenics than in the general population.[13] Among schizophrenics who succumb early in life, this hypothesis seems to hold.) The infectious disease model, the defective nutrition model, and the biochemical model have one useful element in their favor—they are testable—and will soon be found either suitable or unsuitable as sources of further experimentation. There are some models in psychopathology which, despite their heuristic value and despite their great clinical usefulness, have not yet lent themselves to the objective tests which the previously mentioned models afford. The psychoanalytic model, despite its pervasiveness, its acceptance by more than three-quarters of American workers in the field of mental disease and its full-hearted acceptance by anthropology, sociology, and belles-lettres, has achieved few notable victories in science. Its most important contribution perhaps is the catharsis hypothesis for hysteria. The definitions, assumptions, and propositions of the psychoanalytic model have been known for more than fifty years, but not very many experiments have been launched by it. Goshen[6] has already pointed out that though Freud thought he was working with neurotics, actually, most of his cases were psychotic. But his greatest contribution thus far has been for normals. Maybe that is why psychopathology itself has not benefited as much.

Before adding another to the present panoply of models, I shall have to make one detour to examine the possible relationship between personality and psychopathology. Defining personality as the individual's uniqueness, his style of life, or the integrated resultant of all his propensities which singles him out from the rest of mankind, we might raise the question whether the personality of the mental patient is in any way related, premorbidly or postmorbidly to his psychopathology. That his style of life will be affected by the presence of a mental disease is as true of a schizophrenic as it is of a tuberculous patient. But are there any more general statements that can be made about this relationship? Up until now the tacit assumption on the part of some workers has been that a very definite relationship exists. Kretschmer, for example, regards normal behavior as a less extreme and more moderate form of abnormal behavior, thus basing his description of personality on a psychopathological model. But logically there are three possible ways of viewing the connection between personality and psychopathology: (1) that they are identical; (2) that psychopathology emerges from an interference with personality development; and (3) that they are independent of each other. At the present time each of these hypotheses is equally tenable.

Since the hypothesis of independence is in fact the "null" hypothesis, we shall adopt it as our starting point and if the evidence of our investigations contradicts it, it can be discarded. By adopting this model we temporarily discount previous experience encoded in personality as the chief determiner of mental disorders. Instead, we adopt the point of view that current brain function is disordered in a mental illness and seek for techniques which will assay the present state of brain function in the individual. The objective techniques provided by psychophysics and by psychometrics become our chief tools.

It is interesting to note that it was Binet's influence which drove psychophysics out of psychopathology. But Binet's purpose was to study a general aspect of behavior—global intelligence—and for that purpose physiological and psychophysical measures were of little or no help. Our purpose today is to assay the specific capacities of the organism either before illness sets in, or during its early or later manifestations in order to be able to classify individuals with regard to the type of disordered functioning which results when a given mental disease strikes. Elsewhere,[19, 21] I have pointed out how the clinical tests now in use, which are primarily conceptual and heavily dependent on previous experience, fail in dealing with the classification problem.

Here I wish to propose that we return to the time-honored categories of physiological, sensory, perceptual, psychomotor, and conceptual behavior and to experimental ways of eliciting this hierarchy of behaviors.* To some psychopathologists this may seem like turning the clock back to the 1890's but let us listen to one of the "gay nineties" notables speak:

> As soon as our methodology has sufficiently proved itself through experience with healthy individuals, it would be possible to approach the actual ultimate goal of these efforts, the investigation of the sick personality, especially

*For a more basic discussion see Burdock and Zubin.[3]

of the inborn pathological disposition. In an investigation of many individuals we will always find some who deviate profoundly from the behavior of the vast majority in one or another aspect. If this deviation appears to be damaging to the mental life, and if it reaches a certain degree—which admittedly can only be arbitrarily determined—then we tend to regard it as an illness. Experience teaches us that persons with pathological traits of this kind are, on the whole, in greater danger of a general mental disturbance than those personalities (natures) whose characteristics are in the middle range. We therefore have first of all to investigate whether it is possible by means of psychological tests to determine individual deviations, which cannot be recognized by ordinary observation. If that succeeds, we would be in the position, through the quantitative determinations at our disposal, to establish the borderline between health and disease much more precisely and more validly than has been possible so far.[10 p. 77]

This was written not in 1956 but in 1896 by a man named Kraepelin.

Let me now explain the proposed approach. Table 1 shows the five levels of behavior and the techniques for eliciting them.

Physiology is the study of the internal functioning of organisms or parts of organisms, and psychophysiology is often used to designate those variables which have been observed to correlate most closely with observed behavior. These include electrical measurements of the nervous and muscular systems or biochemical assays of the body fluids as the dependent variable, while the independent variable manipulated by the experimenter may belong to any of the stimulus categories.

TABLE 1

EXAMPLES OF MEASURABLE ACTIVITY RELATED TO BEHAVIOR CATEGORIES AND STIMULUS CLASSES

	STIMULUS ORDER			
LEVEL OF OBSERVED BEHAVIOR	0 (IDLING STATE) *S*	I (DISTURBANCES OF HOMEOSTASIS) *S*	II (INAPPROPRIATE STIMULI) *S*	III (APPROPRIATE STIMULI) *S*
CONCEPTUAL	....	ECT; Insulin shock; Lowering of oxygen tension	Electrical stimulation of temporal cortex	Smelling a "sniff set"
R	Reverie and Phantasy	Amnesia, Disorientation, Psychological test performance	Memories Dreams	Recognition of familiar odor
PSYCHOMOTOR	....	ECT	Electrical stimulation of motor cortex	Painful stimulus
R	Spontaneous movement	Seizure	Movement of limb, etc.	Arm withdrawal
PERCEPTUAL	....	Mescal	LSD	Rotating Benham disk
R	Spatial and temporal orientation	Effect on visual orientation	Synaesthesia	Subjective color experience
SENSORY	....	Novocaine	Pressure stimulation above retina; Electrical stimulation of thermal receptors	Light of graded intensity
R	Background noises; cortical gray	Anesthesia	Phosphene warmth or cold sensation	Threshold response
PHYSIOLOGICAL	....	Hyperventilation	Stimulation by implanted electrodes	Photic driving
R	BMR; Basal EEG; Basal PGR	Effect on EEG	Change in blood steroid pattern	Effect on EEG

TABLE 1 (CONTINUED)

LEVEL OF OBSERVED BEHAVIOR	STIMULUS ORDER IV (CONFIGURAL STIMULI) *S*	V (SIGNS) *S*	VI (SYMBOLS) *S*
CONCEPTUAL	Aircraft forms or silhouettes	Classical delayed response stimuli in animal experimentation	Word association test
R	Recognition of identity of forms	Successful response by animal subject	Association to stimulus words
PSYCHOMOTOR	Star-shaped maze	Wagging of tail, nuzzling (dog)	Psychiatric interview
R	Mirror tracing	Petting by human observer	Electromyographic response
PERCEPTUAL	Visual forms	Usual visual alternatives in animal discrimination experiment	Musical tones
R	Discrimination	Selective response of animal subject	Pitch discrimination
SENSORY	Patterned light stimuli	Infant's faint cry	Words or sentences
R	Visual threshold	Mother's auditory threshold	Visual threshold
PHYSIOLOGICAL	Patterned visual stimulation	Bell-ringing in Pavlovian conditioning	Verbal instructions to prevaricate
R	Effect on EEG	Salivation	Effect on PGR

By sensation is usually meant the primitive experience-correlate specific to the stimulation of a sensory-modality. Recent advances in neurophysiology seem to indicate that a sensation is a complex event which in the intact organism includes the following elements:

1. Stimulation of a sense organ or free-nerve ending.
2. Activity of the specific afferent system of a sense organ.
3. Alerting of the organism via the collateral nonspecific afferent system.
4. Small nerve fiber efferent regulation of the sensitivity level of the sense organ.
5. Integration of the afferent and efferent systems at the level of the diencephalon.

Sensation is thus an event in the nervous system involving far-flung activities ranging from the periphery to the cortex, but with the focus of greatest intensity in the thalamus. The occurrence of sensation is detected from behavioral signs displayed by the organism and from concomitant variations observed in the sense organ. With humans, the subject's verbal report is regularly employed as the evidence of his sensory experience. The complexity and subtlety of the experimental situation in which sensory activity is observed are often underrated by an experimenter.

It should be noted that pure sensation is a conceptual abstraction, since sensory activity in most instances merges into perception. Nevertheless, in the study of behavior, the sensory components of activity can be distinguished generally from those which are primarily perceptual. By making a simplifying assumption, the experimenter is thus enabled to set limits to the complexity of his task.

Perception has commonly referred to the process by which patterns are experienced in response to receptor stimulation. The perceptual event appears to involve all of the activity that characterizes sensation with the addition of the large-fiber efferent systems. However, the focus of integration has now moved up to the cortex. Thus, I may have a *sensation* of light, but I *perceive* an object. George Herbert Mead's distinction is worth noting here:

One perceives an object in terms of his response to it. . . . It is true of all of our experience that it is the response that interprets to us what comes to us in the stimulus, and it is such attention which makes the percept out of what we call "sensation." It may well be that the distinguishing aspect of the behavior of an abnormal subject is in his selection of what he will attend to in an experimental situation.[14, p. 114]

Whether attention* is a function which the patient is somehow in control of, turning it on or off in what one might call voluntary fashion or whether there is a sort of automatic screening device which places out of focus or inhibits the registration of inputs that are not prepotent, is an important problem for psychopathologists. Hernández-Peón, *et al.*[8] have observed that in the cat there seems to exist a focus which automatically inhibits a previously ongoing registration of auditory input in favor of a prepotent visual stimulus (mice).

Psychomotor tests evoke from the subject a per-

*As Mead 14, p. 25 has pointed out: "Our whole intelligent process seems to lie in the attention which is selective of certain types of stimuli . . . we open the door to certain stimuli and close it to others, but our attention is an organizing process as well as a selective process. When giving attention to what we are going to do, we are picking out the whole group of stimuli which represent successive activity. Our attention enables us to organize the field in which we are going to act."

ceptual process, including overt movements to which the observer confines his attention. *Perceptual* tests, on the other hand, are aimed at the experience correlative with the patterned activity characteristic of the perceptual event. Thus the distinction between psychomotor and perceptual tests really depends on what the experimenter chooses to scrutinize.

The characteristic feature of *conceptual* activity is the use of symbols* to test the implications of various behaviors in the organism's repertory. The conceptual event probably differs from perception primarily in the complexity and subtlety of cortical elaboration.

When we emphasize the capacity of an organism to form concepts by establishing relations between classes of objects, we are abstracting the end product at which the organism has arrived by a process of symbolic activity. Sign† behavior as the forerunner of symbolic behavior stands on the threshold of conceptual activity. Moreover, the possible complexity of sign behavior should not be underestimated. Thus, in delayed reward experiments, animals respond to a sign which evidences an event remote in time or space. Lower animals probably are limited to relations dependent upon signs. It is for this reason that lower animals are incapable of elaborating complex conceptual

*A *symbol* is a concrete representation for an abstraction from actuality or possibility.[16,p.244] It stands for a map or model of the common elements in a class of related events or their signs. For a definition of *sign,* see the next footnote.

†A *sign* is a representation which is used as evidence for the occurrence of some event. Alternatively, a sign is a symbol whose representation class consists of a single event. For a definition of *symbol,* see preceding footnote.

chains. They are like medieval mathematicians for whom long division was arduous labor because of the Roman numeral system. In man the development of the vocal gesture into a linguistic symbol, socially defined, has made possible the peculiarly human distinction between self and others. According to Mead, this distinction gave rise to the capacity to assume the role of the *other* by implication. From this role-playing, at first limited to social roles, gradually evolved the ability to adopt the role of a nonsocial object.

Each of these categories of behavior can occur in the "idling state," when no controlled stimulation is introduced by the experimenter. The behaviors noted during the idling state at the physiological level and perhaps also on the psychomotor level can often be measured directly, but data on the idling state behavior in the sensory, perceptual, and conceptual spheres can be obtained only retrospectively through interview.

As an example of sensory activity without any controlled stimulation, we might take the background noises which are sensed even when no special attention is paid to auditory stimulation. These background noises seem to have the function of informing the sensorium that the auditory mechanism is working. The severe depression suffered by persons who suddenly lose their hearing has been traced to the elimination of this reassuring information in the sensorium. Perhaps the experience of cortical gray with eyes closed is another example of ongoing sensory activity. The effect of restricted stimulation, as shown by Bexton, Heron, and Scott,[1] dramatically illustrates the importance of the sensory component in complex activity. According to their findings, persons subjected to such "sensory deprivation" usually experience hallucinations. In the light of recent findings relative to efferent modulation of sense organs,[5, 12] these anomalies may correspond to abnormal lowering of threshold. It is as if in the absence of the normal signal, the gain in an electronic amplifier was increased to the point where noise was being interpreted as signal.[17, pp. 118-25] Similarly, the auditory and visual hallucinations and the paraesthesias reported by mental patients disclose to the observer that the sensorium is "out of tune" with the environment.

Perceptual ongoing activity is exemplified by the framework of spatial orientation even when no special attention is paid to the location of objects. Subjective experience of the passage of time is another example. Since schizophrenic patients seem to deviate in spatial orientation and in time judgment, the examination of such ongoing activities is of importance diagnostically.

Ongoing conceptual activities are exemplified by reverie, daydreaming, and phantasy. Deviations in reverie and phantasy are too well known as earmarks of psychopathology to require further mention. It should be realized, however, that these ongoing activities cannot be measured or detected while in process, since the attempt to measure them may interfere with them. The only way we can obtain information on these states is after they have occurred, in retrospect, through interview.

Table 1 gives examples of the idling state for each of the types of behavior in the first column. It also lists various types of stimulation that elicit behavior of differing complexity in controlled experimental situations. A study of the idling state offers evidence of the basal level at which the organism is functioning. Significant variation from the normal idling state may provide evidence of malfunction, as in senescence. It should be noted that the stimulus classes compose a hierarchy in terms of the complexity of the independent variable which the experimenter is manipulating.

This hierarchy ranges from stimuli whose physical parameters alone are sufficient to evoke the observed response to those in which the physical characteristics of the stimulus simply serve as signs or symbols whose properties derive from the previous experience of the individual. S-R relations may also be distinguished as either "energy systems," in which the energy transfer from stimulus to organism is the principal component of observation, or "signal systems," in which the energy of the stimulus simply serves as a trigger to release the intrinsic energy of the response.

Disturbances of homeostasis involve mainly chemical, electrical, or surgical modification of the internal environment. *Appropriate stimuli* are energies within the characteristic sensitivity range of a sense organ, while energies outside of that range are *inappropriate stimuli*. *Configural stimuli* present discontinuous gradations of energy to one or more sense organs. *Signs* and *symbols* involve situations in which the experimenter seeks to evoke a response to the *signal* rather than to the *energy* content of the stimulus.

The attempt to specify the stimulus that evokes a given type of response is, of course, one of the primary problems of psychology.* Indeed, all we really mean when we designate a stimulus is that this is what we have chosen as the independent variable which is to be submitted to controlled variation. Our success in damping out the activity of other "situational" variables is always open to question. We can usually be much surer of the observed response than we are of the alleged stimulus, and we often have to infer the stimulus from the characteristics of the response. Especially difficult is the problem of drawing a line of demarcation between perceptual and sensory stimuli.

Once a controlled stimulus, or stimulating situation, is introduced by the experimenter, physiological activity (bottom row) can be elicited not only by disturbances of homeostasis but by all the other stimulus classes as well. Thus, the EEG will reflect not only brain potentials in the resting state (first column) but also brain potentials under mild hyperventilation (disturbance of homeostasis), under photic driving (appropriate visual stimulation), under conditions of patterned visual stimulation (configural stimulation), and under conditions of problem solving (symbolic stimulation). Conversely, one must remember that a stimulus of one type may elicit responses at all five behavior levels—physiological, sensory, perceptual, psychomotor, and conceptual. In short, both the stimulus classes and the behavior categories comprise transitive hierarchies[3] in which the more complex events include the simpler. In a given experiment, however, the experimenter is usually concerned with

*Klüver's now classic paper[9] presents a comprehensive and incisive discussion of the problem of the equivalence of stimuli.

only one aspect of the response. Thus, the introduction of hyperventilation will probably affect all five levels of response, but in physiological experiments, its effect on EEG alone may be in the focus of attention; while in conceptual experiments, the panic or fear it may induce is what interests the experimenter.

It may very well be that schizophrenics, for example, have different physiological responses from normals. Hence, the introduction of changes in conditions likely to disturb homeostasis is a desirable experimental procedure of psychopathology. It is this field of behavior —the internal milieu of the organism—which has been neglected by many psychopathologists in favor of the interpersonal aspects, a most unfortunate neglect.

In similar fashion, sensory, perceptual, psychomotor, and conceptual behavior can be elicited by the various stimulating situations—disturbances of homeostasis, inappropriate, appropriate, and configural stimuli, and signs and symbols.

In addition to the usual method of eliciting behavior beginning with a subject in the idling state, we might begin the experiment after a stress-producing load had been imposed. These loads could be either of a homeostatic type (drug, temperature increase, etc.); an inappropriate type of stimulation (pressure on the optic nerve); an appropriate type (excessive sensory input or deprivation); configural (patterned auditory stimulation); sign, or symbol (psychological threat). It is quite possible that stimuli administered under a load which taxes the limits of tolerance might reveal deviations in the performance of a schizophrenic which would not otherwise become apparent.

The tentative conclusions which a survey of the literature yields for the various rubrics of this table are as follows:

1. Class of Stimuli
   a) The idling state of mental patients, has offered interesting observations, but not as many as those found when a load is imposed on the idling state.
   b) Homogeneous stimuli, such as those used in eliciting sensory responses, do not yield thresholds which differentiate the mentally ill.
   c) Nonhomogeneous, or patterned stimuli, of the variety used in eliciting perceptual responses indicate a raised threshold for neurotics, even when the sensory threshold in the same modality is normal.
   d) Symbolic stimuli tend to evoke responses in the mentally ill which do not differ in quality from those of normals but only in the degree of communality which they represent.
2. Class of responses
   a) Under a stress-producing load a difference is sometimes found between normals and mental patients, usually in the direction of lower efficiency for the latter.
   b) Under conditions of sensory deprivation, or other types of unloading, absence of the normal braking effect of input noise leads to a disorganization of behavior, probably on all levels—physiological, sensory, perceptual, psychomotor, and conceptual.

Finally, the affective and volitional aspects of psychopathology can be investigated with focused interview techniques in which certain features are manipulated by the interviewer, and assessed by objective methods of content analysis. An example of such an interview is the attempt to condition affective communication by the technique of Greenspoon,[7] and Verplanck.[15]

The first line in each chart shows the cumulative number of affective utterances during the initial stage of an interview before any reinforcement was introduced (operant level). The second line shows the cumulative number of utterances after reinforcement of affective utterances is introduced, by saying "uh huh" or generally agreeing with the patient and encouraging affective utterances while withholding such approval from neutral utterances (conditioning). In the final period, the interviewer returns to the operant level procedure (extinction). Each of these periods lasts ten minutes. Note that the conditioning period invariably results in a steeper slope and a greater number of affective utterances, though considerable individual differences occur. Three different methods of reinforcement were utilized, which we cannot go into at this time, but it is the hope of our research team that some parameters or combination of parameters involved in these curves will remain invariant, transcending the variation in rapport between a patient and different interviewers. If this is found to be true, a measure of flatness, or dullness of affect, useful in prognosis may be evolved.*

*This study is being conducted by Suzan H. Salzinger in connection with Project M-586 C supported by a grant from the National Institute of Mental Health.

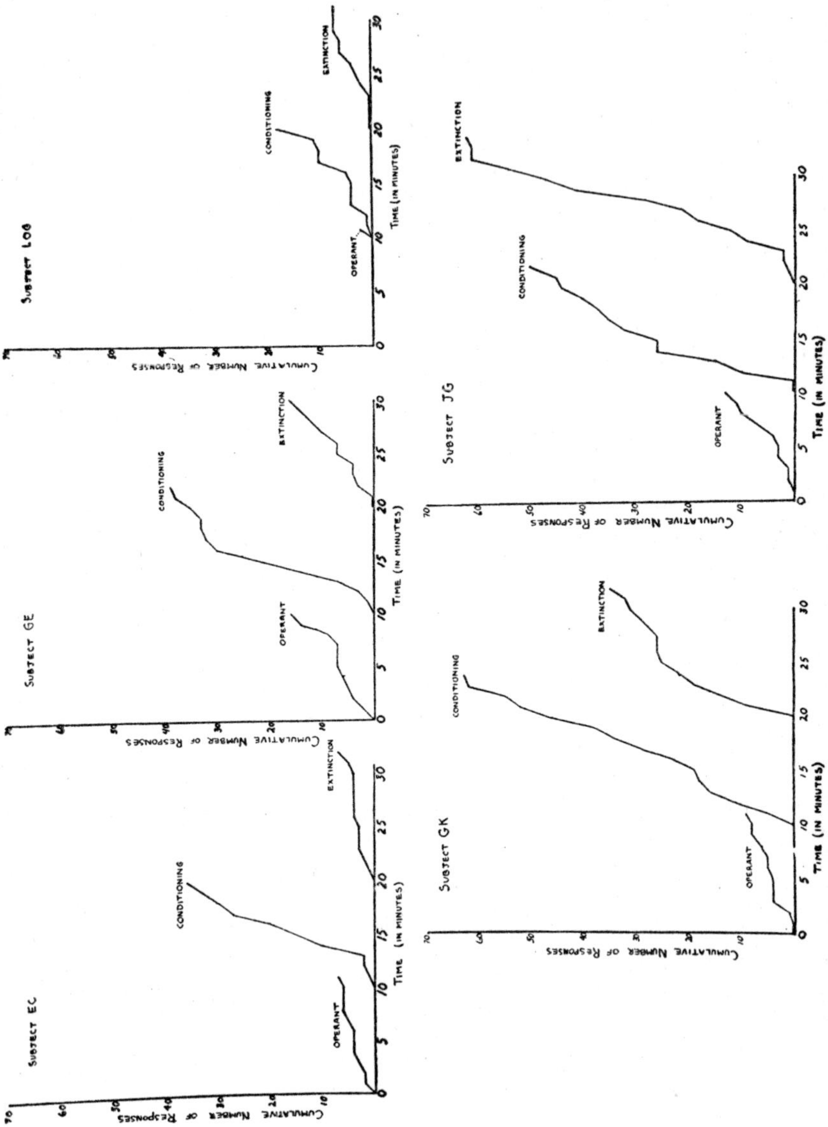

... distribution of affective utterances under three conditions of interviewer behavior.

SUMMARY

The accumulation of isolated facts in psychopathology is impeding rather than accelerating progress, because no suitable models have been proposed for ordering the data. Thus far, the most successful models in psychopathology have been: the infectious disease model, e.g., general paresis; and the nutritional defect model, e.g., pellagra with psychosis. Current research indicates that biochemical models may some day be very helpful in solving the riddle of schizophrenia. The psychoanalytic model has also had its success, e.g., catharsis in hysteria, but has thus far served a heuristic rather than an integrative role. It has been suggestive rather than conducive to further research. One of the difficulties with current models is their tendency to regard the premorbid personality as basic to the development of a mental disorder. The possibility that premorbid personality is independent of the eventual mental disorder, or at best only determines the efforts of the patient in adjusting to the illness, has not been sufficiently explored. If we postulate independence between personality and mental disease, and if we further postulate that disturbed brain function is an important factor or concomitant of mental disorder, we can provide a systematic method for determining the behavioral effects of the disturbed brain function which underlies mental illness. Deviations in the physiological, sensory, perceptual, psychomotor, and conceptual functioning of the patient can be determined under usual conditions, as well as under conditions of a stress-producing load which tests tolerance limits. The affective aspects of behavior can be investigated by means of focused interview techniques, and a content analysis of these interviews can be made in an objective manner. With these two sources of data, the patient population can be diagnosed more objectively, prognostic indicators of outcome promulgated, and the most suitable therapy for each type of patient determined. If this is accomplished, it may be possible to demonstrate that we already have some therapeutic procedures which bring about a degree of improvement greater than that attributable to "spontaneous improvement."

REFERENCES

1. Bexton, W. H., Heron, W., and Scott, T. H. Effects of decreased variation in the sensory environment. *Canadian J. Psychol.*, 1954, 8: 70-76.
2. Bronowski, J. *The Common Sense of Science.* Cambridge, Mass.: Harvard University Press, 1953.
3. Burdock, E. I., and Zubin, J. A rationale for the classification of experimental techniques in abnormal psychology. *J. Gen. Psychol.* (in press).
4. Freundlich, E., von Klüber, H., and von Brunn, A. Ueber die Ablenkung des Lichtes im Schwerefeld der Sonne. *Abhandl. d. Berliner Akad., math.-phys. Kl.*, 1931, p. 35.
5. Galambos, R. Neural mechanisms of audition. *Physiol. Rev.*, 1954, 34: 497-528.
6. Goshen, C. E. The original case material of psychoanalysis. *Amer. J. Psychiat.*, 1952, 108: 829-34.
7. Greenspoon, J. The reinforcing effect of two spoken sounds on the frequency of two responses. *Amer. J. Psychol.*, 1955, 68: 409-16.
8. Hernández-Peón, Raúl, Scherrer, H., and Jouvet, M. Modification of electric activity in cochlear nucleus during "attention" in unanesthesized cats. *Science*, 1956, 123: 331.
9. Klüver, H. The study of personality and the method of equivalent and non-equivalent stimuli. *Charact. Pers.*, 1936, 5: 91-112.

10. Kraepelin, E. Der psychologische Versuch in der Psychiatrie. *Psychologische Arbeiten,* 1896, I, 1-91.

11. Krafft-Ebing, R. Die Aetiologie der progressiven Paralyse. *Arbeiten aus dem Gesammtgebiet de Psychiatrie u. Neuropathologie,* II Heft, 12-12. Leipzig: Johann Ambrosius Barth, 1897.

12. Kuffler, S. W., and Hunt, C. C. The mammalian small nerve fibers: a system for efferent nervous regulation of muscle spindle discharge. *Research Publication of the Association for Research in Nervous and Mental Diseases,* 30, 1952.

13. Lea, A. J. Adrenochrome as the cause of schizophrenia: Investigation of some deductions from this hypothesis. *J. Ment. Sci.,* 1955, 101: 538-47.

14. Mead, G. H. *Mind, Self and Society.* Chicago: University of Chicago Press, 1934.

15. Verplanck, W. S. The control of the content of conversation: Reinforcement of statements of opinion. *J. Abnorm. Soc. Psychol.,* 1955, 51: 668-76.

16. Whitehead, A. N. *Science and the Modern World.* New York: Macmillan Co., 1929.

17. Whitfield, I. C. *An Introduction to Electronics for Physiological Workers.* New York: Macmillan Co., 1953.

18. Wittgenstein, L. *Philosophische Untersuchungen.* New York: Macmillan Co., 1953.

19. Zubin, J. The measurement of personality, *J. Counsell. Psychol.,* 1954, 1: 159-64.

20. ———. On the powers of models. *J. Pers.,* 1952, 20: 430-39.

21. ———. Failures of the Rorschach Technique, *J. Proj. Tech.,* 1954, 18: 303-15.

22. Zubin, J., *et al. Experimental Abnormal Psychology,* Chap. 1. The Scientific Method in Abnormal Psychology (in preparation).

PSYCHOPHYSIOLOGY AND PERCEPTION

DONALD B. LINDSLEY

This work has been supported by USPHS Grant B-362: Mechanism of Vision in Man and Animal. Acknowledgment is also made to a grant from the Carnegie Corporation of New York and an ONR Contract, NONR 233 (32). The following have provided valuable assistance in various phases of the work: Robert W. Lansing, Edward Schwartz, Roy S. Griffiths, and William H. Emmons.

PHYSIOLOGICAL psychology is generally considered to be a search for understanding of the mechanisms underlying psychological processes and the behavior which eventually reflects adaptations and adjustments. While our knowledge along these lines is still very much incomplete, there is considerable understanding of the sensory and motor aspects of the input-output system. Psychophysical and behavioral studies have played a significant role, but in recent years these data have taken on added significance as neurophysiology, and in particular electrophysiology, has gradually unveiled the manner in which receptors and effectors perform as transducers. The broad principles of conversion of physical energy to nerve impulses and the mode of conduction of such messages in sensory and motor nerves is now well known. Thus certain aspects of sensory process and of motor behavior are fairly well understood. What has continued to be a relative void is the nature of central processes involving integration, storage, initiation, and the like. Perception, learning, memory, thought, emotion, motivation, and attention have continued to be happy hunting grounds for theorists.

Reflexology so beautifully and simply demonstrated by Sherrington at the spinal level becomes exceedingly complex in the brain stem. It will not suffice to explain psychological and behavioral events in terms of hierarchies of reflexes. Pavlov, although undoubtedly aware of this complexity, nevertheless sought to simplify the explanations of behavioral modifications in terms of general concepts of cortical function, such as excitation, inhibition, irradiation, and drainage. The compounding of reflex arcs, and the association of one with the other at progressively higher levels, seemed like such a parsimonius way of explaining the complex in terms of the elementary. But it has succeeded in explaining only the grossest and most superficial aspects of behavior. New concepts and ideas are needed, and in part this is what recent neurophysiology has supplied.

During the past ten to twenty years remarkable advances have been made in our understanding of the neurophysiology of the central nervous system. These advances have come through the application of a variety of techniques for the study of the nervous system, but perhaps most significant have been the contributions derived from the procedures of electrophysiology. The techniques of electrical stimulation and electrical recording have made it possible to explore the conditions of electrical excitability, the pathways of conduction from one point to another, and the relationship of nerve impulse volleys to the spontaneous or autonomous electrical activity found among aggregates of nerve cell bodies and their ramifying dendrites.

The work of Adrian,[1,2,3] Granit,[19] and many others, has demonstrated that it is possible to study the manner in which receptors transduce the physical energy supplied by a stimulus to nerve impulses, and how these nerve impulse volleys may be traced along the course of sensory pathways to receiving centers in the brain where they may be localized by their "evoked potentials." Similarly, it has been possible to trace impulse volleys from various motor centers in the brain to their outflow in spinal motor centers and their eventual destination in effector mechanisms. Thus we have a means of tracing, by the electrical signs associated with nerve message transmission, the course of activity from stimulus to response; however, we are still very much in the dark about what happens centrally. We have learned that the telephone system and its central switching mechanism are no longer suitable analogues of our own highly organized nervous systems. Not alone because of the greater complexity, flexibility, adaptability, and differential storage capacities of the brain, but also because the input and output systems are paralleled by ancillary and supporting systems which modify both positively and negatively the effects transmitted in classical pathways. These feed-back mechanisms monitor both input and output transmissions and effects.

It will be impossible to deal here with all of the evidence for these statements, but I should like to mention briefly a few of the general principles which seem to be emerging from neurophysiology and which may have considerable relevance to us in psychology, not only in the interpretation of our psychological phenomena and behavioral data, but I believe also in the future conception of our experimental problems. First, I shall speak of the possible role of parallel input systems, and here I have reference to the classical sensory pathways (primary or specific sensory system) and the reticular activating system (secondary or unspecific sensory system) which receives collaterals from them.

THE ASCENDING INFLUENCE OF THE RETICULAR ACTIVATING SYSTEM

Figure 1 shows schematically upon a phantom projection of a monkey brain the manner in which present evidence suggests the two sensory systems are organized. There is shown an example of a classical sensory pathway, ascending from the spinal cord (or entering at the level of the brain stem if from a cranial nerve), synapsing in the thalamus and proceeding directly to its primary receiving area, in this case the somatic sensory cortex, post-rolandically. Note that this same pathway gives off collaterals (shown by four arrows) in the region of the lower brain stem between medulla and hypothalamus. These collaterals, at the same time the classical pathway is conducting impulses centrally to the thalamus and cortex, feed impulses into the reticular formation which forms the central core of the lower brain stem and contains a network of ramifying neurons. The excitation of these neurons sets up a longer lasting reverberation in the meshwork of fibers and cells composing the reticular formation. Thus a single, brief, stimulus such as a moderately loud click is capable of setting this system in action and the short tegmental relays continue to discharge centrally for some seconds thereafter. Thus this second sensory system adds persistence to the sensory effect upon the higher brain stem and cortex. Note also that the rostral end of the reticular activating system is shown by branching arrows to spread and pervade all areas of the cortex. Thus in contrast to the classical or direct sensory system which is briefly and discretely activated and carries its message to a specific receiving center, the second sensory system or the reticular activating system seems to play another role, characterized by persistence and diffusion of its effects upon the cortex.

What does this second sensory system do? First of all it seems to play a role in the mechanism of sleep-waking.[10, 32, 33] Stimulation of it by direct electrical stimulus, or indirectly by natural sensory stimulus of moderate intensity, will arouse a sleeping animal.[34] Furthermore, such stimulation will shift the electrocortical picture from one of a sleeping pattern with large synchronized waves to one of a desynchronized pattern with low amplitude fast waves of mixed frequency. Similarly in a waking animal, or human, with spontaneous alpha rhythms during a state of quiet relaxation, these waves are blocked or desynchronized by a sensory stimulus which arouses and focuses the attention upon the source of the stimulus. Thus we see that it is a system not only associated with the transition from sleep to wakefulness, but one capable of arousing and maintaining various degrees of wake-

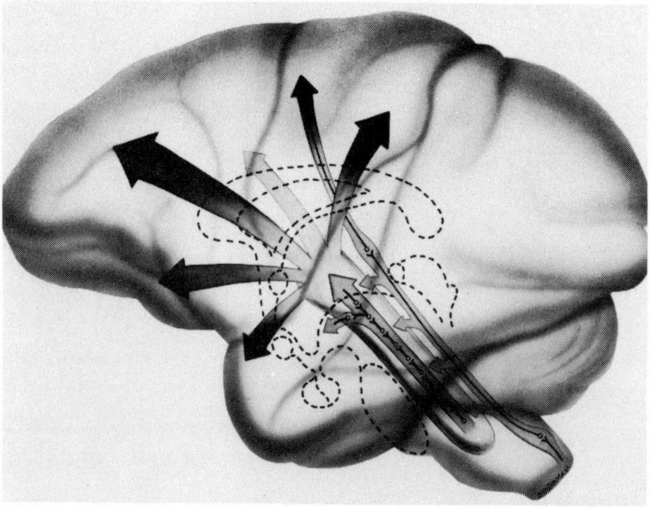

FIGURE 1. Schematic illustration of ARAS (ascending reticular activating system) showing *specific* (primary) and unspecific (secondary) systems on phantom projection of monkey brain. Specific or classical sensory pathway on right after synapse in thalamus goes to a specific location in primary receiving area of cortex. Its messages are brief, discrete, and direct. In region of lower brain stem it gives off collaterals (arrows) to reticular formation consisting of multi-neuronal, multi-synaptic, central core of region from medulla to hypothalamus. The ARAS is comprised of the reticular formation of the lower brain stem and the diffuse thalamo-cortical projections which project widely to all areas of the cortex.

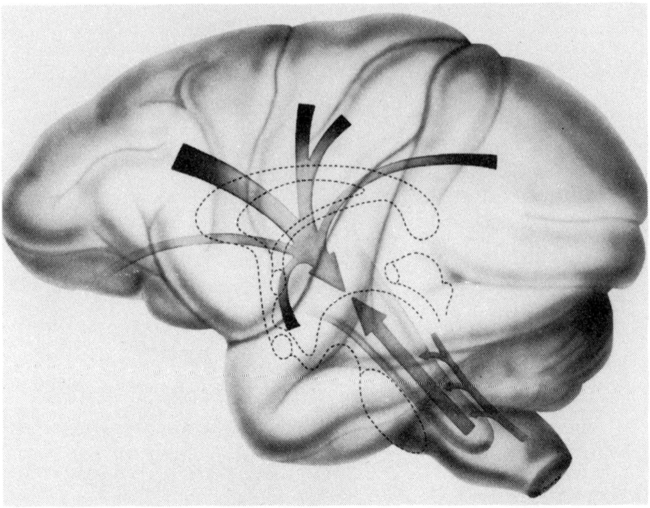

FIGURE 2. Corticifugal pathways and collaterals of classical afferent pathways converging on reticular formation of lower brain stem are schematically illustrated in monkey brain. Stimulation of widespread areas of cortex gives rise to electric potentials in reticular formation hence functional connection by assumed cortico-reticular paths. Thus afferent impulses from all sources and impulses originating in the cortex as result of past experience, learning, ideation, etc., are capable of exciting ARAS, which in turn maintains the cortex (and behavior) in a state of arousal, alertness, and perhaps specifically and selectively attentive. The ARAS probably plays a significant role in drive and motivation also.

fulness or attention. These arousal and alerting functions may be observed in a variety of ways; they may be seen in the electrocortical changes induced in the electroencephalogram (EEG) and in the behavioral states associated with the different EEG patterns (see Table 1).

In cats,[28, 30] monkeys,[16] and man[14] it has been demonstrated that a lesion interrupting the ascending reticular activating system, especially in the rostral midbrain or hypothalamic area, will produce a persisting state of somnolence from which it is difficult to be aroused. This is true despite the fact that the classical sensory pathways (lateral lemniscal pathways of the midbrain) are intact. A strong pinch of the foot or a loud sound may cause momentary signs of arousal such as opening the eyes, raising the head, and so forth, but there is little or no indication that the stimulation is appreciated and the animal immediately returns to a state of somnolence. In those unfortunate human cases, where, after an auto accident or some other injury, there is described a prolonged comatose or somnolent condition, it has been shown that the cause of the extended sleeplike state is pressure impinging upon, or a lesion interrupting at some point in its course, the reticular activating system. Usually this occurs in the tegmentum or reticular formation of the midbrain region.[14]

The role of this unspecific system in perception is suggested by the fact that barbiturate anesthesia will block it, while leaving the specific sensory pathways open.[17] Evoked potentials in response to sensory stimulation may be recorded in the primary receiving areas

TABLE 1

PSYCHOLOGICAL STATES AND THEIR EEG, CONSCIOUS AND BEHAVIORAL CORRELATES*

BEHAVIORAL CONTINUUM	ELECTRO-ENCEPHALOGRAM	STATE OF AWARENESS	BEHAVIORAL EFFICIENCY
Strong, Excited Emotion (Fear) (Rage) (Anxiety)	Desynchronized: Low to moderate amplitude; fast, mixed frequencies.	Restricted awareness; divided attention; diffuse, hazy; "Confusion"	Poor: (lack of control, freezing-up, disorganized).
Alert Attentiveness	Partially synchronized: Mainly fast, low amplitude waves.	Selective attention, but may vary or shift. "Concentration" anticipation, "set"	Good: (efficient, selective, quick, reactions) Organized for serial responses.
Relaxed Wakefulness	Synchronized: Optimal alpha rhythm	Attention wanders —not forced. Favors free association.	Good: (routine reactions & creative thought).
Drowsiness	Reduced alpha and occasional low amplitude slow waves.	Borderline, partial awareness. Imagery & reverie. "Dream-like states."	Poor: (uncoordinated, sporadic, lacking sequential timing).
Light Sleep	Spindle bursts and slow waves (larger) Loss of alphas.	Markedly reduced consciousness (loss of consciousness) Dream state.	Absent
Deep Sleep	Large and very slow waves (synchrony) but on slow time base) Random, irregular pattern.	Complete loss of awareness (no memory for stimulation or for dreams).	Absent
Coma	Isoelectric to irregular large slow waves.	Complete loss of consciousness little or no response to stimulation; amnesia.	Absent
Death	Isoelectric: Gradual and permanent disappearance of all electrical activity.	Complete loss of awareness as death ensues.	Absent

*From Lindsley (26)

of the cortex indicating that conduction over the classical sensory pathways is intact; the sensory messages thus apparently get to the cortex, but whatever is required for their integration is absent since the animal or human does not respond to these messages in any meaningful way. Hence without the reticular activating system it appears that discrimination is not possible; also the electrocortical activity is not desynchronized by sensory stimulation as is characteristic when the reticular system is intact. Evidence of its ability to facilitate the handling of incoming impulse volleys by the cortex will be described later in this chapter.

DESCENDING INFLUENCES OF CORTEX UPON RETICULAR SYSTEM

Not only do impulses from sensory sources feed into the reticular activating system and arouse and alert the animal; it has been shown additionally that stimulation of certain areas of the cortex produce evoked potentials in the reticular formation.[15] Thus there is provided the possibility of feed-back control, possibly both negative and positive in character. In the case of negative feedback it is assumed that there would be control and regulation of the degree of activation, such as might be necessary under conditions of strong pain, stress, and emotional arousal. There could also be a tempering influence of past experience and learning, since we know these operate in the control of behavioral reactions. With respect to positive feedback it appears that the cortical effect of reinforcement associated with past habit formation could increase the discharge from cortex to reticular formation and in turn further activate the organism to respond. Essentially this is what we have come to know as motivation. In the human positive feedback might be the central effect of "set" or "instructions" to perform in a certain way or put forth a given amount of effort. We might think particularly of the effort to pay attention or to stay awake when a critical task is at hand. At least it now appears that a suggested cortical-reticular mechanism or pathway is at hand to explain the phenomena and types of behavior we are familiar with in every-day experience.

Figure 2 illustrates the relatively diffuse cortical origins of such feed-back control to the reticular activating system. Here, then, is one more mechanism by means of which sensory input may be regulated. Other recently demonstrated feed-back regulations at the level of the receptor, the spinal, and the relay centers have been reviewed elsewhere.[27]

Initially it was thought that both the ascending reticular activating system and the descending cortical feed-back connections to it operated rather diffusely and not selectively or differentially. More recently it has been shown[21] that the effect of the unspecific system may extend to the primary sensory areas in differential manner as well as to the associated fields. It has also been demonstrated by microelectrode technique that individual units of the reticular formation may be activated differentially by different stimuli.[5,36] Although it still appears that the over-all effect of stimulation through single- or multi-sensory channels is to produce a generalized effect upon electrocortical activity and to serve as a general arousal or alerting mechanism, there is now some reason to believe that differential excitation of the system is possible. This would, of course, provide for greater flexibility of control, and might conceivably account for the phenomenon of selective attention. Thus it appears that the reticular activating system, or the second sensory system, as it is sometimes called, provides the mechanism by means of which it may be possible to explain a number of psychological phenomena heretofore well known, but not understood.

NEUROPHYSIOLOGY OF PERCEPTION

With this brief background account of a new conception of parallel sensory input systems and a feedback control mechanism for regulating or modifying input, I should like to turn now to some experimental observations on a specific sense modality. Three years ago I began work upon the visual system mainly because it seemed to be an excellent avenue of approach to the brain. I was less interested in vision per se than in the effects of external visual stimuli upon the central nervous system and their relations to the "spontaneous" alpha rhythm of the cortex. It had already been shown that "photic driving" of these rhythms was possible.[4, 37, 38, 41]

No specific function of the alpha waves of the electroencephalogram (EEG) has ever been found, although it has been suggested[6, 8, 12, 26] that they may indicate a waxing and waning excitability of local neurons giving rise to them. Such an hypothesis has seemed worth attempting to test even though there are many difficulties involved. Several studies[31, 35, 39, 40] dealing with the alpha rhythm as a possible scanning mechanism have attempted to verify this concept, but mainly without success. However, the *scanning* and *excitability* concepts are not mutually dependent upon one another, and neurophysiological evidence for the latter has been sufficient to provide encouragement for further investigation. A study done in my laboratory by Lansing[22] has provided evidence favoring the excitability concept, and will be described later in connection with some special views about the role of the alpha rhythm.

An attempt has been made to plan parallel investigations in human and animal subjects. Using time-limited visual stimuli the limits of perception determined psychophysically in human subjects have been compared with the limits of evoked responses in the visual pathways and cortex of cats and monkeys. By this cross-species comparison of human subjective judgment with the electrical responses in the visual system of animals it has been possible to obtain some interesting correlations and establish some similarities of function. Our most recent work, now in progress, involves implantation of electrodes in the visual pathways and cortex of cats so that behavioral observations and electrical recording may be carried on simultaneously in the same animal. These are called "chronic" preparations, as opposed to the "acute" preparations upon which the work reported here is based.

The procedure for studying electrical potentials in the visual system of the cat (or monkey) at various stations from the eye to the cortex simultaneously in an acute preparation is as follows. The animal is anesthetized deeply with ether and its trachea is cannulized for artificial respiration when needed. The animal is then placed in a Horsley-Clarke stereotaxic instrument, a device which permits the localization of points deep in the brain in terms of their rectangular coordinates. Since we wish to work with an unanesthetized brain, a transection (or electrolytic lesions) is made in the midbrain region, after the manner of the cerveau isolé preparation of Bremer.[11] Our transection is made just caudal to the inferior colliculus at an angle calculated to eliminate all sensory influx to the brain, except impulses via the olfactory and visual systems. Cut surfaces of the scalp and pressure points are injected with procaine hydrochloride to insure that any sources of pain impulses are eliminated. Thereafter, ether anesthesia is discontinued. Holes are drilled in the skull, or portions of the skull are removed in order to permit entry of deep electrodes and placement of electrodes upon the visual area and other control areas of the cortex. Wick electrodes are placed on either side of the bulbus of the eye for recording the electroretinogram (ERG). Needle electrodes are placed in the optic nerve, optic tract, lateral geniculate bodies, and optic radiations by means of the Horsely-Clarke instrument (Johnson). Cortical electrodes of the wick or ball-tipped type are positioned and held in place by a Grass cortical electrode holder adapted for use with the monkey and cat. As electrodes are lowered to their respective stations in the visual system, electrical recording during single or multiple flashes of light introduced into the pupil, which is dilated with homatropine, insures by the nature of the response obtained that the electrode tips are in the optimal position. Later after the day's experimentation is complete, the animal is sacrificed and its brain is perfused and fixed in formalin. After hardening, the brain is sectioned and stained and observed under microscopic projection so that the track of the electrodes and the exact location of their tips may be identified in the visual structures for which they were destined.

Figures 3 and 4 show two views of a monkey prepared as described above. The side view in Figure 3 shows the monkey in the Johnson-type Horsley-Clarke stereotaxic instrument with all electrodes in place, ready for recording. The monkey and the instrument are placed in a black, light-tight box, which is covered with copper screening and grounded, thus forming an electrical shield against unwanted extraneous influences. The door comprising the side of the box hangs down open. Light generated by a photoflash device or other source passes through a monochromator for limited band wave lengths and is brought to a focus at the eye. Part of the beam is diverted to a photocell the output of which is amplified and fed back to the recording instrument for indicating the incidence of the light upon the eye. In the figure it will be noted that the light passes through a small tube with a shield in front to prevent stray light from entering the eye or affecting recording electrodes photochemically. The electrode holder directly above the eye holds the electrodes which go to the eye and which lead off the electrical potentials (ERG) generated when the flash of light falls upon the retina. The wires directly above the head of the animal go to electrodes in the holders of the stereo-

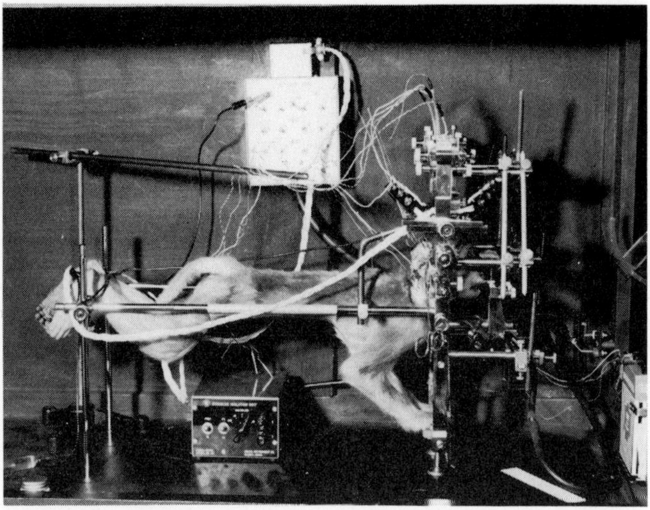

FIGURE 3. Monkey in Horsley-Clarke stereotaxic instrument (Johnson) in light-tight and electrically shielded box. Light stimuli project from optical system on right to dilated eye of monkey. Electrodes on eye record electroretinogram (ERG); those in holder of instrument are lowered into brain in terms of rectangular coordinates and are destined for optic nerve, optic tract, lateral geniculate body, and optic radiations; those at back rest on surface of exposed cortex. Single or repetitive light flashes may be given and electrical responses recorded simultaneously from several stations along the visual pathways from eye to cortex.

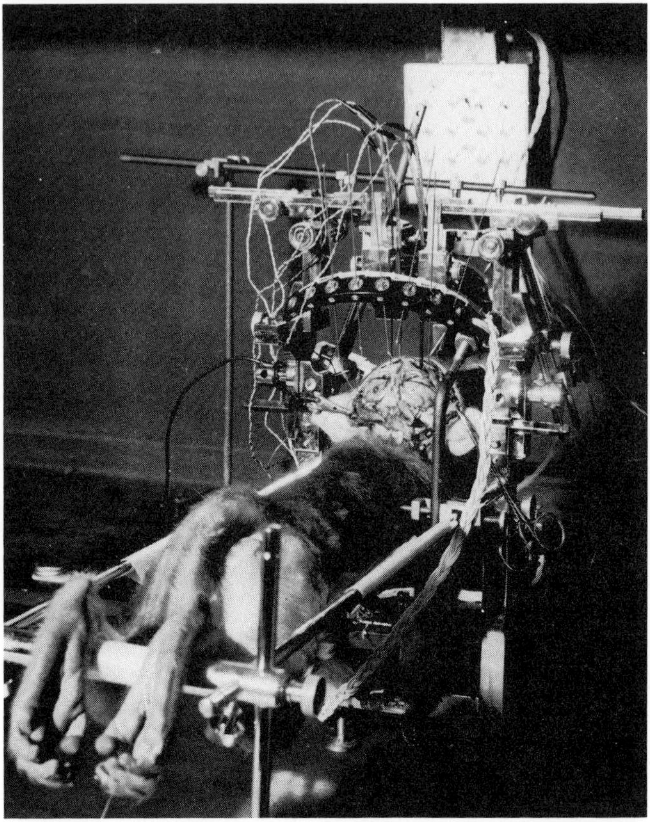

FIGURE 4. Rear view of monkey in Horsley-Clarke instrument showing exposed visual cortex, with wick electrodes located on different regions. Rods holding wicks are adjustable in ball and socket joints in special electrode holder.

taxic instrument which are destined for the optic nerve, optic tract, lateral geniculate body, and the optic radiations. The electrode holder behind and above the head contains several electrodes which impinge upon the exposed visual cortex, or other non-visual control areas. All of these electrodes attach at the white plug-in box at the rear of the box and are led through a shielded cable to the amplifying and recording instruments, where EEG inkwriter-type records, optical oscillograph, or cathode-ray oscillograph recordings may be made. On the floor beneath the monkey is a stimulus isolation unit which is connected to an electronic stimulator outside the box and which may be used to introduce electrical stimulation into various brain sites when desirable. For example, electrodes are often placed in the reticular formation of the lower brain stem for purposes of activation by external electric stimulus. As a later record will show, this has proved to be an effective means of modifying the response of the cortex to impulses arriving over the visual pathways. Note that a syringe is attached to plastic tubing indwelling in the femoral vein for purposes of intravenous injection. Often Flaxedil, a curare-like compound, is introduced to eliminate reflex motor movements by blocking impulses at neuromuscular junctions. Figure 4 shows a rear view of this preparation, with visual cortex exposed bilaterally.

Figure 5 illustrates some typical electrode positions upon the cortex of the cat, and projected drawings of histological sections through the diencephalon showing the path and end point of needle electrodes in optic tract (OT) and lateral geniculate body (LG).

Cortical leads 1, 2, and 6 are resting on the surface of the cortex over visual area I and area II; leads 4 and 5

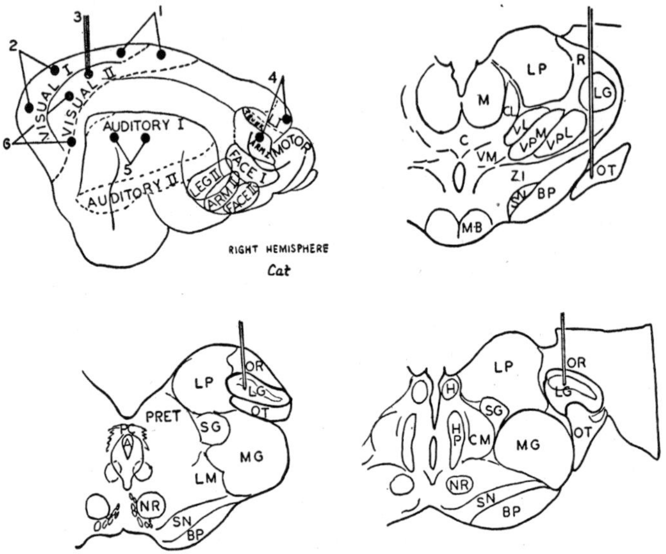

FIGURE 5. Schematic outline of lateral surface of cat brain showing typical arrangement of electrodes on visual I and II areas, and control, nonvisual areas. After experimental data are collected, brain is removed and histological sections prepared for locating exactly position of electrodes; these are magnified, projected and traced. Upper right section shows path of electrodes to optic tract; lower right section a few millimeters posterior in diencephalon shows electrodes in lateral geniculate body; lower left section still farther posteriorly shows another pair of electrodes in lateral geniculate. Key: *MB,* mammillary bodies; *OT,* optic tract; *OR,* optic radiations; *NR,* nucleus ruber; *BP,* basis pedunculi; *SN,* substantia nigra; *ZI,* zona incerta; *PRET,* pretectal region. Thalamic nuclei: *LG,* lateral geniculate; *MG,* medial geniculate; *LP,* lateralis, posterior; *VM,* ventralis medialis; *VL,* ventralis lateralis; *CL,* centralis lateralis; *M,* dorsalis medialis; *CM,* centre medianum; *VPM,* ventralis postero-medialis; *VPL,* ventralis posterolateralis.

are over somesthetic and auditory cortex, respectively; concentric leads 3 have a tip one millimeter in the visual cortex and the shoulder of the external lead rests on the surface of the cortex. Sample sections of the brain through the region of the diencephalon are shown from anterior (upper right) to posterior (lower left). The two bottom sections show electrodes in different parts of the lateral geniculate body; the upper right section shows electrodes in the optic tract. Unless the electrodes penetrate the visual structure concerned, no electrical response is recorded when a flash of light is introduced into the eye; on one occasion or more an electrode destined for the lateral geniculate missed its mark and ended up in the adjacent medial geniculate body (MG), the relay nucleus for auditory impulses, and though the tips of the electrodes were no more than one millimeter removed from the visual structure (LG) no response was recorded to visual stimulation, thus indicating little or no spread within the nervous tissue of the thalamus.

In order to understand the variations in electrical responses recorded from the various visual structures it seemed desirable to study the effects of each of the stimulus parameters such as intensity, duration, wave length, light/dark ratio, area, and frequency of repetitive flashes of light. Time does not permit my dealing with each of these variables and the type of response recorded in each of the stations along the visual pathways. These data will be published elsewhere. I shall concentrate here upon only a few of the features which seem to have parallels in human perception. One of these is the *frequency* of repetitive light flashes and the

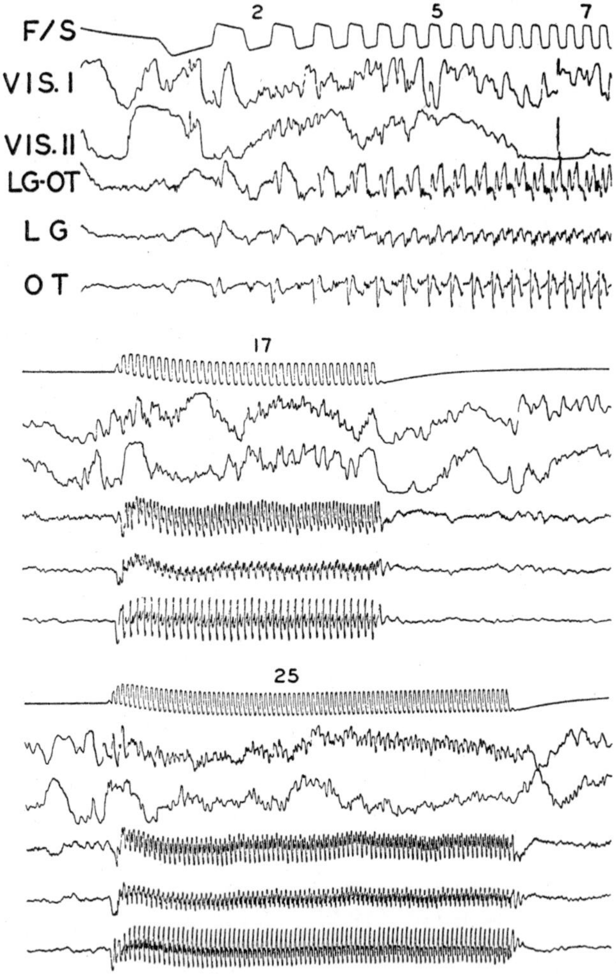

FIGURE 6. Multiple EEG inkwriter recordings from various stations in visual system of cat during repetitive visual stimulation. From top down: *F/S,* flashes per second—photocell response; Vis. I, visual cortex I; Vis. II, visual cortex II; *LG-OT,* margin lateral geniculate and optic

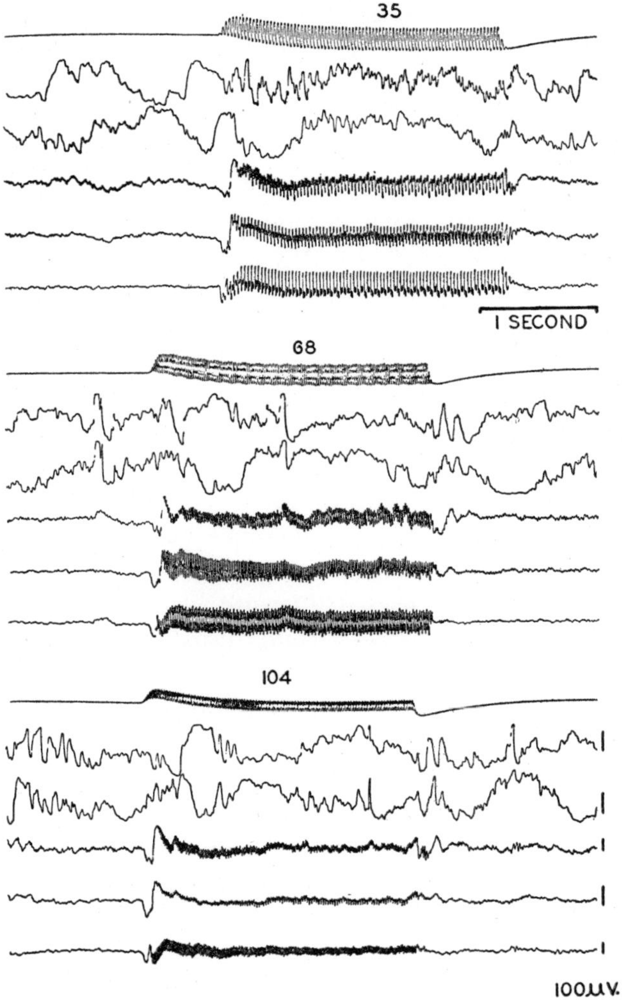

tract; *LG,* lateral geniculate; *OT,* optic tract. Optic tract and geniculate responses follow flash rate over 100 per second; cortex follows to about 45 per second only. Note one to one following of flashes by Vis. I at 25 and 35 per second.

relation of the responses in the visual pathways and cortex of animals to the apparent counterpart of this as manifested in human perception by critical flicker frequency (c.f.f.).

Figure 6 shows the electrical responses in the optic tract (OT), lateral geniculate body (LG), the junction of lateral geniculate and optic tract (LG-OT), area II visual cortex (Vis. II), and area I visual cortex (Vis. I). The top line shows the response of the photocell to the repetitive light flashes at different rates or flashes per second (F/S). In the visual pathways, each flash of light gives rise to a discrete response (usually both on and off components are visible) as may be seen in the optic tract and lateral geniculate records. This is true also in the cortex for the lower frequencies, but "spontaneous" activity sometimes obscures the response. Visual cortex I shows a good following response at 25 flashes per second; likewise, at 35 per second. Between 35 and 68 per second (usually 40 to 45 per second for this intensity) the cortex stops following the individual flashes of light, but the optic tract and lateral geniculate body continue to give discrete responses, flash by flash, to well over 100 flashes per second. It appears therefore that the cortex (or possibly the postsynaptic neurons of the lateral geniculate) constitutes a limiting factor in the response to repetitive light flashes. Since the point of failure for this intensity of light is about 45 per second, and since for the average human subject c.f.f. is about 42 per second for the same light intensity it appears that c.f.f. may be due to a limitation of the cortex, rather than to the peripheral mechanism of the eye or the visual pathways.

So much for one parallel between human perceptual limits and the limits of electrophysiologic response in the cortex of the cat (and monkey).

A second parallel may be observed when two very brief flashes of light are presented in quick succession to the human and to the cat. If two 10 microsecond flashes are presented to a human subject, separated by 150 or 100 milliseconds, he will see them as two. If they are separated by 50 milliseconds, he will see them as one. His psychophysical judgment for this threshold separation of flashes will be about 70 milliseconds for a given intensity of light.[29] In the cat or monkey, two flashes by the same light separated by 150 or 100 milliseconds produce two distinct evoked potentials at the visual cortex, but when the flashes are 50 milliseconds apart only one evoked potential is recorded. This is illustrated in Figure 7. It will be observed that the response to two flashes 50 milliseconds apart is similar to that for a single flash, whereas flashes separated by 100 or 150 milliseconds give two similar responses. Thus again there appears to be a parallel between the limits of human subjective judgment in resolving two flashes of light and the limits of response of the cortex.

At this point it may be well to introduce another observation which emphasizes a possible role of the second sensory system, or the *ascending reticular activating system* (ARAS) mentioned earlier. While recording electrical responses in the cat's visual system to two flashes of light as described above, it was found that electrical stimulation of the reticular formation changed the visual cortex response from one evoked potential per pair of flashes to two. Figure 8 illustrates this effect. Pairs of flashes 50 milliseconds apart were presented once per second and each time the visual cortex (VC) (shown in the bottom trace) gave one evoked potential. Then the reticular formation was stimulated for 5 seconds (3 volt, 1 msec. pulses, 300 per second). Immediately after reticular stimulation ceased, and for the next ten seconds, each pair of flashes

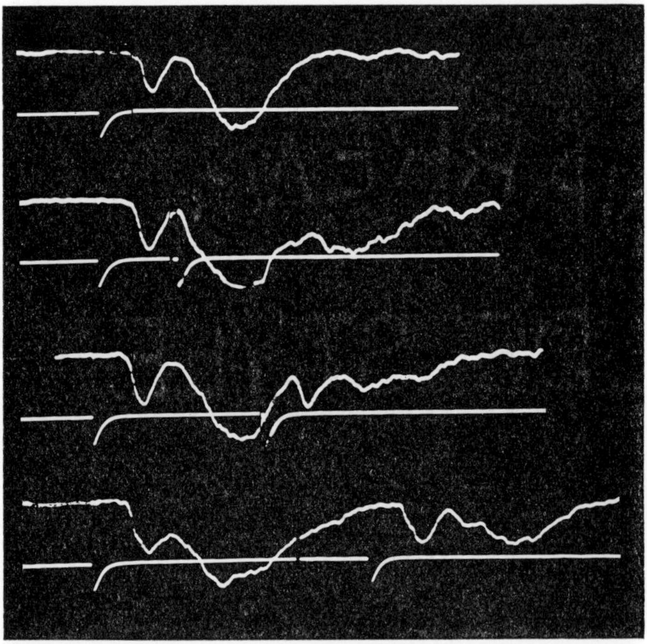

FIGURE 7. Cathode ray oscillograms of evoked potentials in visual cortex of cat showing double response to pairs of brief light flashes separated by 100 and 150 milliseconds (bottom two tracings), but single response to one flash (top record) and to two flashes 50 milliseconds apart (second from top). Human subjects see 50 millisecond pairs as one; 100 and 150 millisecond pairs as two; cat's cortex seems to respond similarly.

now evoked two responses in the visual cortex. Thereafter the response reverted to its original state with only one evoked potential per pair of flashes. This indicates that the ARAS had a facilitating effect upon the cortex and its resolving power for time-limited stimuli. It suggests that the reticular formation and the unspecific sensory system represented by the ARAS is capable of playing a role in perception. As will be discussed later, we know that any sensory stimulus, and particularly novel or unexpected stimuli, are capable of setting the ARAS in action. Subjectively and behaviorally we speak of the effect or state created by such stimulation as one of increased attention or alerting. We know that human discrimination ability is improved by "set" or attention, established by instructions, or a warning signal of an impending discrimination to be made. The experiment illustrated by Figure 8 suggests that it is the cortex which is facilitated in this process. Although in this instance the reticular formation and the ARAS was set in action by an electrical stimulus directly applied, we know that it may be set in action by sensory stimuli from visceral or somatic sources, and likewise from corticifugal pathways. Presumably it is through the demonstrated cortico-reticular functional connections described earlier (see Figure 2) that ideation and past experience play a role in establishing "set" or enhanced attention, which as we have seen increases the efficiency of the cortex to resolve incoming messages.

When the ARAS is stimulated, whether by direct electrical stimulus, or by natural sensory stimulation, we may observe its effect upon the electroencephalo-

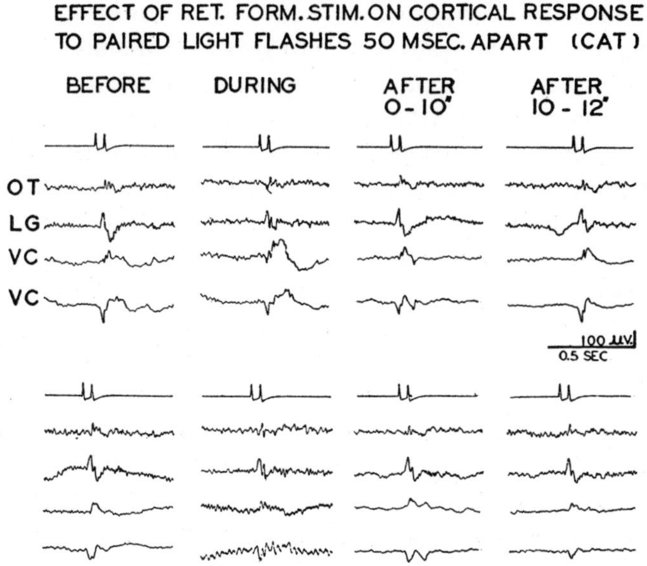

FIGURE 8. Responses in cat's optic tract *(OT)*, lateral geniculate *(LG)*, and visual cortex *(VG)* to pairs of light flashes 50 milliseconds apart. Note in lower *VC* record, *one* evoked potential prior to reticular stimulation, and *two* responses for 10 seconds after reticular stimulation. After 10 to 12 seconds response reverts to single evoked potential. Shows effect of ARAS in increasing resolving power of cortex by facilitation.

gram and the brain rhythms so recorded. As Moruzzi and Magoun[34] demonstrated, direct electric stimulation of the reticular formation in the cat changed the electrocortical picture from one of a sleeping state with synchronized slow waves and spindle bursts to a desynchronized picture composed of low amplitude fast waves of mixed frequency. They also demonstrated that an auditory or a tactual stimulus produced a similar change. In a waking, but relaxed animal with rhythmic, synchronized waves of lower amplitude, a sensory stimulus tends to desynchronize or block the so-called alpha waves and leave a relatively flat tracing or one with low amplitude fast activity on it. The same is well known to electroencephalographers with regard to the human EEG, which blocks or desynchronizes when a sensory stimulus is presented which attracts the attention of the subject. In the following section observations bearing on the EEG and particularly the role of the alpha rhythm will be given.

ROLE OF THE ALPHA RHYTHM OF THE EEG

Berger,[7] in 1929, published the first paper on the human electroencephalogram (EEG). In a series of subsequent papers he described changes in the EEG associated with various psychological, physiological, and pathological states. He identified the alpha rhythm (8 to 13 per second waves), and the much smaller and more rapid beta waves (20 to 50 per second). Others confirmed and extended his observations. The details may be found in various reviews,[13, 20, 25] and many additional sources will be found in Brazier's bibliography.[9]

Despite many valuable uses to which the EEG has been put, both clinically and experimentally, we still do not know the precise origin of one of the outstanding features of it, the alpha rhythm. There is little doubt of its cortical origin and of its autochthonous nature, since undercut and isolated cortex is capable of generating such a rhythm. But where among cortical neurons these rhythmic potentials arise cannot be said with certainty. Whether the potentials are a product of activity in dendrites, cell bodies, or both is still a moot question. Microelectrode studies suggest that there are two types of activity which can be recorded in the vicinity of individual cortical neurons, a slow rhythmic activity of the order of an alpha rhythm, and a spikelike potential characteristic of neuronal discharge. According to Li and Jasper,[24] the former do not depend upon the latter, and may be associated with membrane potentials. If this latter concept is true, it might suggest that the spike discharges of a unit would be dependent upon the phase of the slow potentials which would signalize a waxing and waning state of excitability of the neuron. In order to record an alpha rhythm over a region composed of many thousands of neurons it would be necessary for the slow potentials of individual units to synchronize in a rhythmic beat based on the fundamental rhythm of the unit. Impulses arriving in the cortex over the specific sensory pathways do not apparently disrupt this rhythm, but the associated effects of the unspecific or secondary sensory system, via the ARAS and diffuse thalamo-cortical projection system, disrupt and desynchronize it in a widespread manner. In fact, it is this action of a secondary nature which appears to make perception possible, for under barbiturate anesthesia when the reticular formation is suppressed, but the classical, specific, sensory pathways are still capable of conducting impulses to primary receiving areas where they elicit evoked potentials, there is no perceptual discrimination. The ARAS seems to be necessary for the elaboration and integration of sensory messages, and it presumably accomplishes this by desynchronizing the alpha rhythm of larger areas beating homogeneously and creating a more differentiated state of the cortical matrix. In this state individual neurons still have their characteristic alpha activity, but are dynamically interactive with smaller aggregates than before. The differential phase relations of these aggregates or subaggregates, according to the hypothesis, places them in different stages of excitability. Therefore, incoming impulses via specific projection paths may or may not find a given aggregate ready to respond.

Figure 9 is an attempt to illustrate schematically how this process of differentiation leads to greater speed and efficiency of processing of incoming information. We will start with a fact well known in electroencephalography. During a state of relaxation and rest in the absence of special stimulation, a rhythmic 10 per second alpha rhythm is characteristic of the average normal adult. When he is given a problem to solve, or becomes highly attentive to a novel or unique stimulus, the EEG assumes a desynchronized form and is composed of low amplitude fast activity, as in the case of ARAS activation. Such EEGs are illustrated, and it is assumed that these patterns could be produced by brain fields of homogeneous or differentiated nature, respectively, as illustrated on the right of the figure. If we assume further that the peak of the alpha waves in the resting state is the phase of excitability of the neurons giving rise to it and drop a vertical line below, we see that 10 times per second the entire domain of cells in the brain field alternates states of excitability with inexcitability. Using the same principle with each of the rhythms from the differentiated aggregates which are not in phase with one another, it will be seen that the periods of excitability are nearly continuous in time. This would suggest that one aggregate or another is in a state of readiness to response to incoming sensory messages. The predicted result

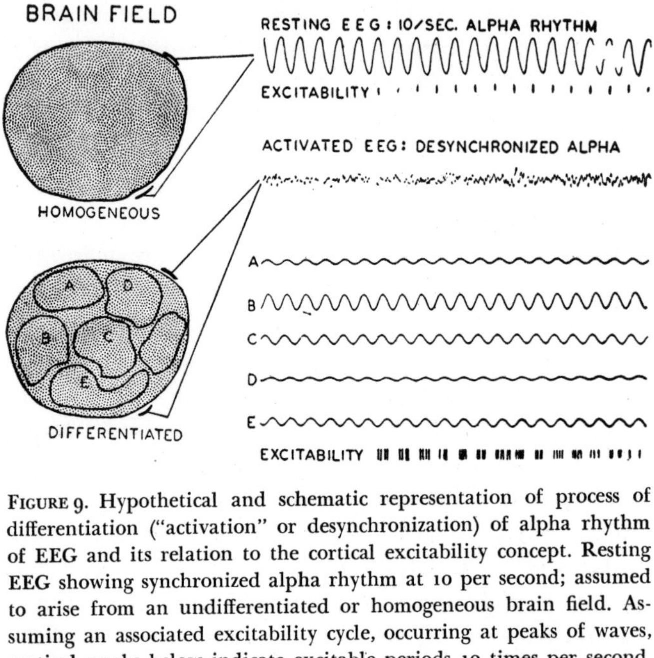

FIGURE 9. Hypothetical and schematic representation of process of differentiation ("activation" or desynchronization) of alpha rhythm of EEG and its relation to the cortical excitability concept. Resting EEG showing synchronized alpha rhythm at 10 per second; assumed to arise from an undifferentiated or homogeneous brain field. Assuming an associated excitability cycle, occurring at peaks of waves, vertical marks below indicate excitable periods 10 times per second. The "activated" EEG is believed to be a desynchronization of alpha activity arising from a differentiated brain field with various dynamically changing aggregates of neurons responsible for alpha rhythms which tend to be out of phase with one another, as shown by *A, B, C, D, E,* etc., tracings. Vertical marks dropped from each of peaks result in almost continuous excitability of one or another of the cellular aggregates, thus favoring speed and efficiency of processing incoming messages. The activated or differentiated EEG is characteristic of a problem-solving state or state of alertness or attention.

is greater speed and efficiency of processing the messages. Empirical data verify the fact that faster, more efficient, behavior occurs during an alerted, desynchronized, or differentiated state of the EEG, as opposed to the rhythmic alpha pattern of the relaxed nonalerted state. The highly speculative explanation in terms of brain fields and excitability cycles simply provides a vehicle for further thought about the mechanism, and generates new ideas to be put to test. Several kinds of hypotheses have been generated in terms of the concept of excitability cycles, and two of these will be dealt with here.

The first has to do with reaction time to a simple visual stimulus, and why the time of reaction varies so widely, for example, from perhaps 150 to 250 milliseconds or more. On the basis of the excitability concept it was argued that 100 milliseconds or more of variation in reaction times might be due to delays encountered by impulses arriving in receiving or association areas in an unfavorable phase of the excitability cycle. Actually, such a cycle might well exist in thalamic relays, in the motor cortex, or in the anterior horn cell pool of the spinal cord. Lansing[22] studied this problem in my laboratory by recording occipital alpha waves, motor area alpha waves, finger tremor waves of the responding finger, and related the incidence of the visual stimulus to the occipital alpha wave phase, and the response to the motor alpha wave phase. Figure 10 shows typical records. Since the visual stimuli were presented at random during periods of good alpha rhythm, they fell in different phases of the wave. Likewise, the phase of the motor wave in which

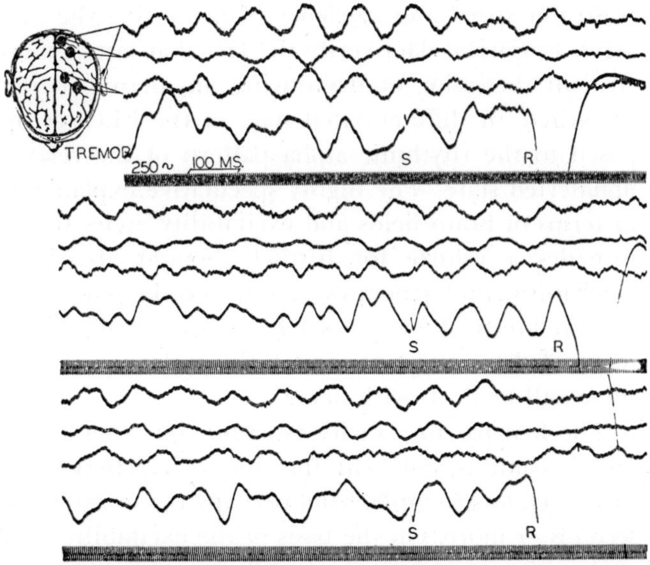

FIGURE 10. Relation of brain and tremor rhythms to reaction time. Stimulus *(S)* onset related to phase of occipital alpha wave (top trace) and Response *(R)* of finger related to motor area alpha wave (third from top), and phase of tremor rhythm (fourth from top). For briefest reaction times stimulus occurs in given phase of occipital alpha wave, for longer ones, elsewhere. Similarly, for motor response and motor alpha wave. Response tends to occur on descending phase of tremor wave. (From Lansing, 22.)

the response occurred was noted. It was found that for the briefest reaction times the stimulus tended to occur in a given phase of the occipital alpha wave, and the motor response fell in a given phase of the motor area alpha wave. When each of these were corrected, respectively, for latency from eye to cortex, and from motor area to finger movement, it was found that they fell in the same phase of their respective areal rhythms, thus favoring the excitability cycle concept.

Since in the foregoing study good alpha waves were required, no attempt was made to alert or activate the subjects. Instead, they were given instructions to respond as quickly as possible, but to remain relaxed. In a subsequent study[23] an attempt has been made to create two conditions, one, a nonalerted state with good, poor, and no alpha waves, and two, an alerted state with a forewarning auditory signal at different intervals prior to the visual stimulus. Figure 11 illus-

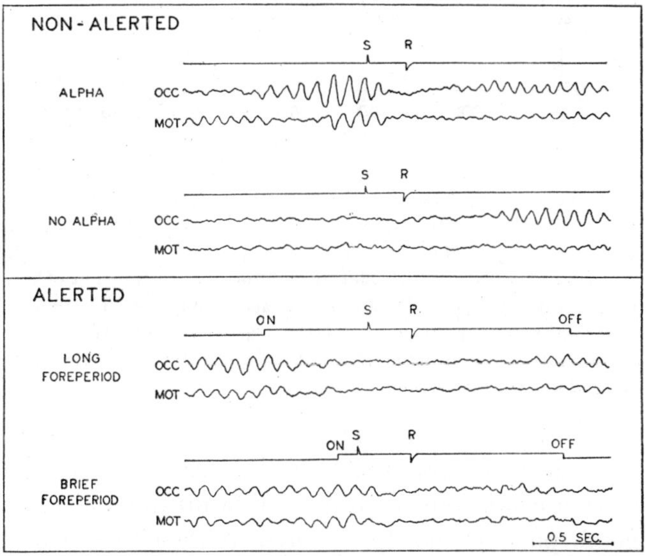

FIGURE 11. Measurement of visual reaction time under nonalert (with and without alpha waves present) and alert (brief forewarning by auditory signal and long foreperiod) conditions. Note in brief foreperiod that alpha waves are not yet blocked when visual stimulus occurs, whereas they are blocked in the case of the long foreperiod thus indicating activation. (From Lansing, Schwartz, and Lindsley, 23.)

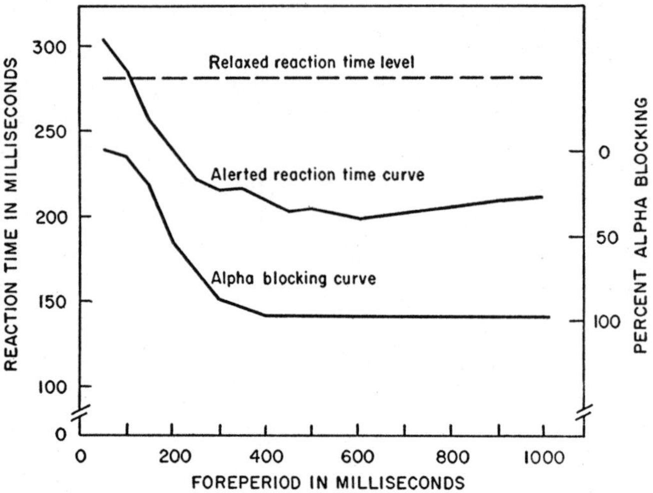

FIGURE 12. Plot of reaction time as a function of foreperiod warning; note that major reduction has occurred by three- to four-tenths of a second, although still more reduction goes on until about six-tenths of a second. The other curve shows the per cent of alpha blocking (per cent of trials in which blocking complete) as a function of foreperiod warning; note that blocking or activation occurs by three- or four-tenths of a second, and therefore activation via ARAS corresponds rather closely with the resulting reduction in reaction time. (From Lansing, Schwartz, and Lindsley, 23.)

trates the conditions. The results show that reaction time averages about 280 milliseconds in the non-alerted conditions, with no significant differences for good, poor, or no-alpha states. With a forewarning of 50 to 250 milliseconds, which was short of the usual three- to four-tenths of a second required by a stimulus to desynchronize the alpha waves, the reaction time was reduced to 255 milliseconds; with a longer period of forewarning (300 to 1,000 milliseconds) permitting alpha blockade prior to the visual stimulus, reaction time was reduced to 206 milliseconds. The curve of reduction of reaction time (see Figure 12), as a function of the length of the forewarning period of activation, parallels that of the per cent of completeness of blocking or desynchronization. Hence it seems that alerting or activation via the ARAS, as indicated by the EEG desynchronization, is correlated with a reduction in reaction time as a function of the length of the forewarning period.

Another type of experiment with which we have been concerned is illustrated in Figure 13. For letters, or for a clocklike geometric figure, we have done psychophysical thresholds for the duration of perception.

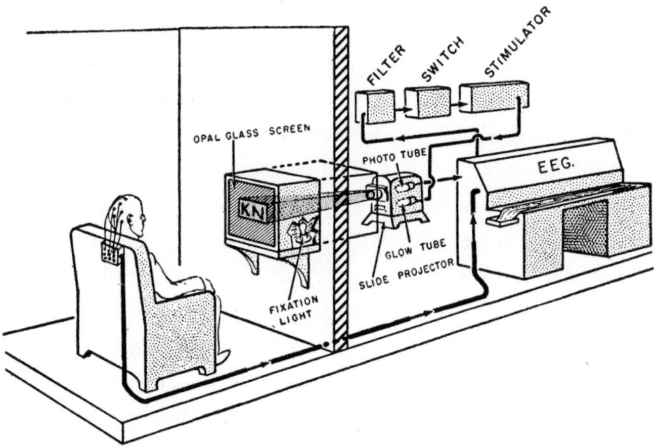

FIGURE 13. General layout for perceptual duration experiments, monitored by EEG recording. Subject seated in dark room with image to be perceived projected on masked opal glass screen by glow modulator tube, tachistoscopic projector for varying duration. EEG recording of alpha wave peak may serve as trigger for a projected flash placed at any time in subsequent alpha wave cycle. (From Schwartz, Lansing, Emmons, and Lindsley.)

On the average, the threshold turns out to be about 5 milliseconds. As in the case of any threshold, one might well ask why is it seen (or heard, or felt) 50 per cent of the time only, if a person is able to see it at all. It has occurred to us that the excitability cycle postulated in relation to the alpha rhythm might be part of the answer. For example, the stimuli are presented at random in the course of time, and relative to the ongoing alpha rhythm. If the onset of the stimulus, after a suitable latency for conduction time to the region of the receiving or association cortex responsible for the alpha rhythm, occurred during an inexcitable phase no response would occur; whereas, if the impulses from a succeeding stimulus arrived during an excitable phase of the alpha wave, the stimulus would be perceived. In this way one might account for a threshold, particularly where duration of the stimulus is involved. An intensity threshold would involve additional factors such as excitation of a greater number of fibers, a larger volley and more prolonged train of impulses, but might be subject to the same excitability factors at the cortical level. To better test this hypothesis, the threshold duration stimulus has been presented in a time relationship to the alpha rhythm which can be adjusted as desired. For example, a device activated by the peak of an alpha wave triggers an electronic device capable of setting in a measured delay-interval of 10, 20, 30, 40 milliseconds, etc., after which it triggers the glow modulator tube of the tachistoscopic projection apparatus. Thus the image to be perceived at a threshold duration may be so placed in time as to fall at any given point in an alpha wave cycle. We have done some experimentation along these lines, but the data are not yet completely analyzed. The object was to find out whether a brief, threshold-duration presentation given at the right point in time relative to the alpha wave excitability cycle would be perceived more often than 50 per cent of the time. One serious loophole in such an experiment is the fact that excitability cycles associated with spontaneous rhythmic activity may exist at several stations on the input side, whereas we are measuring them in relation to one site only. With electrodes on the scalp over the visual association areas, our precision and accuracy of sampling is probably not very great. As in the case of Lansing's reaction time study, however, it may provide us with some evidence favoring the excitability concept.

One might ask how "activation" or "alerting" by means of a preliminary warning signal would affect perceptual duration thresholds, keeping in mind that reaction times were markedly reduced under such ARAS influence. This type of study, using the EEG as a monitor, we intend to do. A very interesting study of this type has been done with monkeys by Dr. Joaquin Fuster, a visiting scientist from Spain, who has been working in the UCLA laboratories. Dr. Fuster has kindly permitted me to report very briefly upon one aspect of his studies. Figure 14 shows the basic arrangements for the experiment. A monkey is trained to find a food reward under one of two objects, in this case a pyramid-like, flat-sided cone and a smooth-sided cone; thereafter he is brought before test apparatus with an opaque screen and a one-way vision

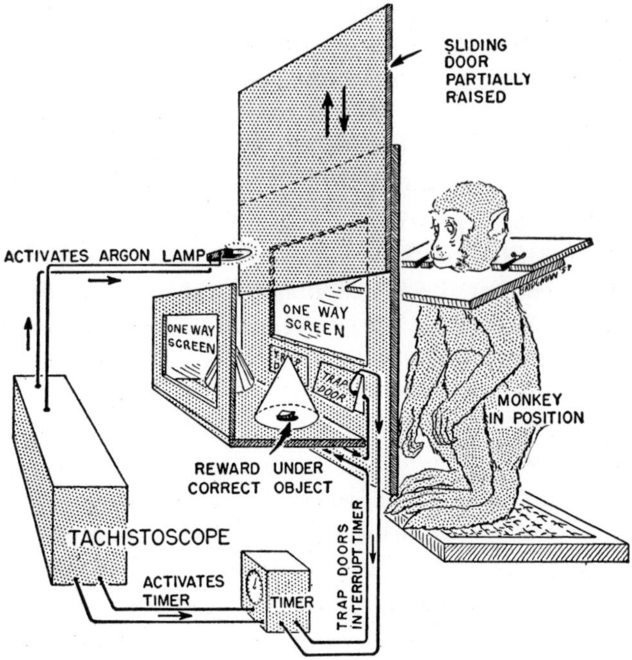

FIGURE 14. Tachistoscopic reaction time in monkey. Flash duration varied to measure perceptual duration reaction time and accuracy. Monkey trained to discriminate test objects, then subjected to tachistoscopic exposures. Light flash starts timer and monkey reaching through trap door after choice stops timer, giving visual perceptual reaction time. Monkey wears a yoke to prevent reaching implanted electrodes in reticular formation and other regions of brain. (By courtesy Dr. Joaquin Fuster, UCLA Medical School.)

screen separating him from the test objects. The opaque screen is raised, but the monkey cannot see the test objects until an argon, tachistoscopic flash light illuminates the figures. The duration of this flash may be regulated. When the flash illuminates the figures, a timing device is started, the monkey observes the figures and makes his choice and reaches through a small door opposite the selected figure. This action stops the timer, thus giving a reaction time for visual perception. Electrodes chronically implanted in the reticular formation of the monkey's brain permit electrical stimulation during the testing.

Figure 15 shows some typical results obtained by Dr. Fuster.[18] Each animal serves as his own control. The curves on the left of the figure are for percentage

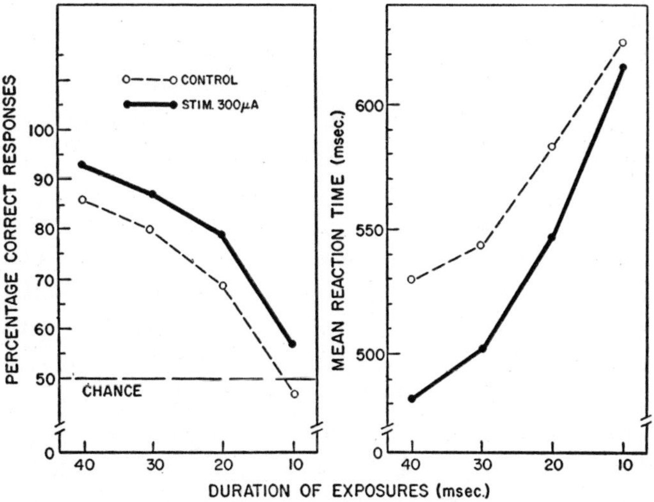

FIGURE 15. Graphs showing percentage of correct responses and mean reaction time as functions of the duration of exposure of stimulus objects before monkey. Normal control tests show per cent correct response decreases and reaction time increases as exposure interval is reduced; 10 milliseconds is approximately a threshold duration. When the same monkey is stimulated electrically by implanted electrodes in reticular formation during test trials the per cent correct response is raised at all durations, and the reaction time is reduced. (By courtesy Dr. Joaquin Fuster, UCLA Medical School.)

of correct response at each of the exposure durations; the dotted or control curve shows a decreasing per cent of correct response as duration decreases. A duration of 20 milliseconds gives about 70 per cent correct responses, whereas 1 of 10 milliseconds duration falls below chance level. The solid curve represents the trials during reticular stimulation, and it will be seen that the per cent correct responses were raised at all durations. Each of the points on the curves represents 100 trials. On the right of the figure the reaction times, as a function of the duration of exposure, are plotted for control conditions and for reticular formation stimulation. It is clear that reticular stimulation increased the efficiency with which the monkey responded, since reaction times at all durations are decreased. These results are comparable to ours, previously mentioned, where nonalerted and alerted reaction times were measured in relation to the EEG which served as a monitor for activation, desynchronization, or differentiation, depending upon how one wishes to describe the effect. In Fuster's experiment the reticular formation was stimulated directly, but artificially, by electrical pulses; in our experiment the ARAS was presumably activated by an instructional "set" triggered by an auditory stimulus serving as a cue for the "set." In both experiments the effect was the same, namely, a reduction in reaction time; however, Fuster's experiment involved a difficult perceptual discrimination. Thus we have seen two examples, in different species, where the ARAS has facilitated or speeded up perceptual and reaction time processes; we have also described for the cat a greater facilitation of the cortex for handling time-limited impulse discharges arising from brief pairs of flashes separated by 50 milliseconds. How much the human threshold for discrimination of a pair of lights barely seen as two might be reduced by suitable activation has not yet been studied, but in terms of other parallels between human subjective thresholds and the electrophysiologic limits of response in the cat or monkey one might predict that the human two-flash or critical interval threshold would be reduced by stimulation or set affecting the ARAS.

SUMMARY

The study of behavior and psychological phenomena has proceeded successfully for many years, but with very little or inadequate understanding of the central neural mechanisms involved. This has been due partly to a lack of sufficient comprehension of such mechanisms, and partly to an unwillingness to seek out and utilize such information as has been available. It has seemed inevitable that the time would come when a fuller knowledge of central nervous system functions would be not only a necessity, but would assist appreciably in the formulation of problems and the design of experiments in psychology. A closer liaison between psychology and neurophysiology, and a fuller interaction and exchange of information would seem to be desirable for progress in both fields. Recent advances in neurophysiology and the development of new concepts of brain function have given impetus to new approaches in physiological psychology. The thesis of this paper has been to try to show how interaction and collaboration between psychologists and neurophysiologists might be beneficial to both.

Among recent developments in neurophysiology which appear to have significance for psychology are some new insights into brain organization. Perhaps foremost of these is the ARAS, or ascending reticular activating system, which plays a prominent role in the mechanism of *sleep-waking*. In addition, combined information from neurophysiology, neuroanatomy, electroencephalography, and psychology suggests that the ARAS plays a significant part in *general arousal* or *alertness*, and perhaps also in *specific alerting* or *selective attention*. Of major significance in relation to each of these phenomena, which are obviously of importance to psychology, is the reticular formation which forms the central core of the lower brain stem and extends from the medulla into the diencephalic region, with diffuse projections to the cortex. When the reticular formation is excited by impulses of sensory origin which reach it by way of *collaterals from the classical sensory paths* in the lower brain stem, or by impulses originating in the cortex which appear to reach it by *corticifugal or cortico-reticular paths,* it affects the electrical activity of the cortex in a diffuse way. It causes synchronized and rhythmic waves to disappear and in their place there is a low amplitude, fast, activity, often described as "activation" because it seemingly activates or desynchronizes cortical activity and also tends to activate or change behavior, for example, from sleep to waking, from waking to alert, attentive states, and so forth.

The ARAS constitutes a kind of second sensory

system, since it derives its excitation from sensory sources. But it also may be excited from the cortex, and in this sense it serves both as a feed-back control mechanism and as an initiator of activity. In both of these instances it would seem to play a role in drive and motivation, because it assists in the initiation of activity and also has a persistent quality, not shared to the same extent by the messages reaching the brain from classical afferent pathways. Furthermore, when the reticular formation is blocked by barbiturate anesthesia, even though messages via classical paths appear to reach the cortex as usual, as indicated by evoked electrical potentials, it appears that perceptual discrimination cannot take place. Hence the ARAS seems to have a significant role in perception.

Some of the experiments described employ a parallel approach in human and animal subjects, and have permitted a comparison between limits of psychophysical judgments of flicker-fusion, critical interval for discriminating two flashes from one, perceptual duration, and so forth, and electrical responses in the visual pathways and cortex of cats and monkeys. The correspondence between the two sets of data, perceptual in one case, and electrophysiological in the other, suggest not only a similarity of the processes, but perhaps an identity of the mechanisms. These experiments are based upon time-limited phenomena, that is, the critical limits, of perception, or of the cortex, or other relevant structures, for responding to certain time intervals of short or limited duration.

Finally, it has been demonstrated in both human and animal subjects that such limits may be extended by appropriate stimulation of the reticular activating system, either by electrical stimulus directly, as in the animals, or by sensory stimulation, or the establishment of a "set" by instructions and a stimulus cue, which served as an alerting stimulus in the human subjects. Thus facilitation, by the reticular activating system, of sensory perceptual processes seems to have been demonstrated. That inhibition and control through some of these mechanisms is also a possibility seems to be implied from recent data. Not only does it appear that facilitation and inhibition are possible through feed-back controls from the cortex to the reticular formation, but that these may assume specific and directional form begins to appear likely as well. The specific mechanism for these more elaborated and specialized functions is only beginning to unfold.

BIBLIOGRAPHY

1. Adrian, E. D. *The Basis of Sensation.* London: Christophers, 1928.
2. ———. *The Mechanism of Nervous Action.* Philadelphia: University of Pennsylvania Press, 1932.
3. ———.*The Physical Background of Perception.* Oxford: Clarendon Press, 1947.
4. Adrian, E. D., and Matthews, B. H. C. The Berger rhythm: Potential changes from the occipital lobes in man. *Brain,* 1934, 57: 355-84.
5. Amassian, V. E., and DeVito, R. Unit activity in reticular formation and nearby structures. *J. Neurophysiol.,* 1954, 17: 575-603.
6. Bartley, S. H. Temporal and spatial summation of extrinsic impulses with the intrinsic activity of the cortex. *J. Cell. Comp. Physiol.,* 1936, 8: 41-62.
7. Berger, H. Über das Elektrenkephalogramm des Menschen. *Arch. Psychiat. Nervenkr.,* 1929, 87: 527-70.

8. Bishop, G. H. Cyclic changes in excitability of the optic pathway of the rabbit. *Amer. J. Physiol.*, 1933, 103: 213-24.

9. Brazier, M. A. B. *Bibliography of Electroencephalography*. Supplement No. 1, *EEG Clin. Neurophysiol.*, 1950. (Montreal: *The EEG Journal*)

10. Bremer, F. The neurophysiological problem of sleep. In *Brain Mechanisms and Consciousness,* pp. 137-62. Oxford: Blackwell, 1954.

11. ———. Cerveau isolé et physiologie du sommeil. *C. R. Soc. Biol.* (Paris) 1935, 118: 1235-42.

12. Chang, H.-T. Cortical response to stimulation of lateral geniculate body and the potentiation thereof by continuous illumination of retina. *J. Neurophysiol.*, 1952, 15: 5-26.

13. Ellingson, R. J. Brain waves and problems in psychology. *Psychol. Bull.*, 1956, 53: 1-34.

14. French, J. D. Brain lesions associated with prolonged unconsciousness. *A.M.A. Arch. Neurol. Psychiat.*, 1952, 68: 727-40.

15. French, J. D., Hernández-Peón, R., and Livingston, R. B. Projections from cortex to cephalic brain stem (reticular formation) in monkey. *J. Neurophysiol.*, 1955, 18: 74-95.

16. French, J. D., and Magoun, H. W. Effects of chronic lesions in central cephalic brain stem of monkeys. *A.M.A. Arch. Neurol. Psychiat.*, 1952, 68: 591-604.

17. French, J. D., Verzeano, M., and Magoun, H. W. A neural basis of the anesthetic state. *A.M.A. Arch. Neurol. Psychiat.*, 1953, 69: 519-29.

18. Fuster, J. M. Tachistoscopic perception in monkeys. *Fed. Proc.*, 1957, 16: 43. (To be published.)

19. Granit, R. *Receptors and Sensory Perception*. New Haven: Yale University Press, 1955.

20. Jasper, H. H. Electrical signs of cortical activity. *Psychol. Bull.*, 1937, 34: 411-81.

21. Jasper, H., Naquet, R., and King, E. E. Thalamocortical recruiting responses in sensory receiving areas in the cat. *EEG Clin. Neurophysiol.*, 1955, 7: 99-114.

22. Lansing, R. W. "The Relationship of Brain and Tremor Rhythms to Visual Reaction Time." Ph.D. thesis, University of California at Los Angeles, 1954. (A condensed version accepted for publication in *EEG Clin. Neurophysiol.*, 1957.)

23. Lansing, R. W., Schwartz, E., and Lindsley, D. B. Reaction time and EEG activation. *Amer. Psychologist,* 1956, 11: 433. (To be published.)

24. Li, C. L., and Jasper, H. H. Microelectrode studies of the electrical activity of the cerebral cortex in the cat. *J. Physiol.,* 1953, 121: 117-40.

25. Lindsley, D. B. Electroencephalography. In Hunt, J. McV. (ed.). *Personality and the Behavior Disorders,* Chapter 33, pp. 1033-1103. New York: The Ronald Press Company, 1944.

26. ———. Psychological phenomena and the electroencephalogram. *EEG Clin. Neurophysiol.,* 1952, 4: 443-56.

27. ———. Physiological psychology. *Ann. Rev. Psychol.,* 1956, 7: 323-48.

28. Lindsley, D. B., Bowden, J. W., and Magoun, H. W. Effect upon the EEG of acute injury to the brain stem activating system. *EEG Clin. Neurophysiol.,* 1949, 1: 475-86.

29. Lindsley, D. B., and Lansing, R. W. Flicker and two-flash fusional thresholds and the EEG. *Amer. Psychol.,* 1956, 11: 433. (To be published.)

30. Lindsley, D. B., Schreiner, L. H., Knowles, W. B., and Magoun, H. W. Behavioral and EEG changes following chronic brain stem lesions in the cat. *EEG Clin. Neurophysiol.,* 1950, 2: 483-98.

31. MacKay, D. M. Some experiments on perception of pattern modulated at alpha frequency. *EEG Clin. Neurophysiol.,* 1953, 5: 559-62.

32. Magoun, H. W. An ascending reticular activating system in the brain stem. *A.M.A. Arch. Neurol. Psychiat.,* 1952, 67: 145-54.

33. ———. The ascending reticular system and wakefulness. *In Brain Mechanisms and Consciousness,* pp. 1-20. Oxford: Blackwell, 1954.

34. Moruzzi, G., and Magoun, H. W. Brain stem reticular formation and activation of the EEG. *EEG Clin. Neurophysiol.,* 1949, 1: 455-73.

35. O'Hare, J. J. The variability of auditory and visual reaction time with change in amplitude and phase of alpha rhythm. *Amer. Psychol.,* 1954, 9: 444.

36. Scheibel, M., Scheibel, A., Mollica, A., and Moruzzi, G. Patterns of convergence and interaction of afferent impulses on single units of the reticular formation. *J. Neurophysiol.,* 1955, 18: 309-31.

37. Toman, J. Flicker potentials and the alpha rhythm in man. *J. Neurophysiol.,* 1941, 4: 51-61.

38. Walker, A. E., Woolf, J. I., Halstead, W. C., and Case, T. J. Mechanism of temporal fusion effect of photic stimulation on electrical activity of visual structures. *J. Neurophysiol.*, 1943, 6: 213-19.

39. Walsh, E. G. Visual reaction time and the alpha rhythm: An investigation of a scanning hypothesis. *J. Physiol.*, 1952, 118: 500-508.

40. Walter, W. G. The functions of electrical rhythms of the brain. *J. Ment. Sci.*, 1950, 96: 1-31.

41. ———. *The Living Brain*. New York: W. W. Norton & Company, Inc., 1953.

ON THE USE OF DRUGS IN THE ANALYSIS OF COMPLEX HUMAN BEHAVIOR WITH EMPHASIS ON THE STUDY OF MOOD

VINCENT NOWLIS

The nondrug work on mood described in this talk is supported by contract N6onr–241, T. O. V (Responsible investigator–V. Nowlis) between the University of Rochester and the Group Psychology Branch of the Office of Naval Research. The drug work has been supported by a contract between the University of Rochester and the Office of Naval Research, N6ori–126, T. O. I (Responsible investigator–G. R. Wendt), by grant M-681 from the National Institutes of Health (Principle investigators–H. H. Nowlis, V. Nowlis, and G. R. Wendt) and by grants from S. D. Searle and Company and other sources.

INTRODUCTION

THERE has been recently a tremendous increase in the use of drugs in behavioral research. This increase is based on developments like the following: (1) military interest in the side effects of drugs which might be selected for such purposes as mitigating motion sickness or fatigue and boredom or pain; (2) use of tranquilizing drugs in the management of psychiatric and medical patients; (3) use of drugs as aids in psychotherapy; (4) experimental production with drugs of psychotic-like states and the inhibition of such effects with other drugs; (5) increased dissatisfaction of anesthesiologists with some of their traditional beliefs;

(6) increased pressure to understand psychological dependence on widely used drugs; (7) advances in neurophysiology and neuro-pharmacology; (8) the availability of certain drugs which might give the research psychologist, not otherwise interested in studying drug effects, a means for controlling factors in his experimental analysis of behavior. This paper is addressed to psychologists in this last category, for my thesis today is simply that at the same time that all this research on sheer drug effects is going on, experimental psychologists can profitably begin to use certain drugs in an attempt to control or systematically change factors relevant to basic psychological problems. In other words, psychologists who are strongly involved in certain research problems may sooner or later find it useful to know that certain drugs bring about certain effects. Solomon,[18] for example, brilliantly utilized curare in his ongoing studies of conditioning. For reasons which are somewhat obvious, but which merit a discussion later on, such work by researchers not primarily interested in drug work itself will nevertheless contribute to the scientific evaluation of drug effects as well as to a science of behavior.

Since we need to recognize some common loci within which both drug research and basic psychological research can profitably interact, reviews of the expanding literature on drugs must be written for the research psychologist. The present paper is not such a review. In this connection, B. F. Skinner and Peter Dews organized a symposium at the New York Academy of Science on May 4, 1956, with the topic of techniques for the study of the behavioral effects of drugs.

After four years of collaboration in research with the effects of drugs on college men, the locus in which I have become interested involves the concept of mood and the experimental analysis of the antecedents and consequents of mood change. In the first place, change in report of mood is one of the important behavioral changes following the administration of certain drugs. Secondly, it has recently been found that something like mood change is important in a most promising research area in social psychology, the area of communication and persuasion. Hovland, Janis, and Kelley[9] and Janis and Feshbach[10] recently have shown that the presentation of communications designed to arouse fear elicits verbal report of feelings of anxiety and that this change in emotion or mood is important in understanding the effectiveness of the communication in changing opinions.

The first section of this paper will present a sample of the Rochester drug work. The second section will present an attempt at an objective definition of mood. The third section will discuss the control of mood in research on communication and persuasion.

A SAMPLE OF THE DRUG RESEARCH AT ROCHESTER

Since 1951, G. R. Wendt, Helen Nowlis, and I, with our collaborators, particularly A. H. Riesen, under the sponsorship of the Office of Naval Research, the United States Public Health Service, the G. D. Searle Company, and the University of Rochester, have studied the effects of mild dosages of drugs such as amphetamines, anti-histamines, and barbiturates on the behavior of college men in experimental group sessions.

A total of about ninety-five men have been observed in approximately 2,400 hours of controlled social interaction and in about 4,800 hours of relatively free activity. Moderate doses were always used, producing effects well within the range of nonmedicated variation applicable to the individual during, say, any one month or year. Our subjects were not often certain that they had had a drug. Sometimes they were certain that they had had a drug when they were on placebo. Strong doses are inappropriate for various reasons, an important one being the confounding of the drug effect with strong reactions to the compelling symptoms of a strong dose.

Each of the ninety-five carefully screened college men has gone through a procedure like the following for from four to eighteen times. Four of the men reported at noon to our comfortable, somewhat isolated laboratory, which was equipped with large, one-way vision mirrors and with high-fidelity sound recording. They ate a standard lunch, gave a self-report of their mood on a check list of from 100 to 200 adjectives. During two years the subjects had an individual administration of the Gehl-Kutash Grapho-motor Test at this time and three hours later. On a desk beside their conference table was a pile of blue envelopes, each of which was labeled according to a time schedule. In the envelopes were instructions about each of their experimental tasks, various check lists, and blanks for partner- and group-ratings; also in the envelopes were the standard white capsules which they took orally at a designated time. Neither subject nor observer knew the contents of the capsule. Time to open each envelope was indicated by a buzzer controlled by an observer. Throughout the three-hour session the men were alone. During the first hour they performed on from three to five tasks, involving such activities as the French four-man ball-and-spiral task, discussion of dilemmas or current issues, assembly of lumber or of words, the four-man electro-maze, and a fifteen-minute rest period. Drug was taken during this first hour at a time selected to have onset symptons during the immediately following hour of free activity and to have steady state during the final experimental period, or third hour. During this final experimental period tasks equivalent to those of the first hour were performed. By 4:00 P.M. the men were ready to rest; by 5:00 P.M. they had decided which downtown restaurant they would descend on; during the evening they returned to the laboratory for study or recreation, according to individual or group choice. At 10:00 P.M. they were escorted to their regular residences where they remained, under pledge to stay home and do no drinking. No accidents have occurred during these years. We are satisfied that it is feasible and proper to do carefully supervised drug research with college men of appropriate age and character. Each year we have more and more spontaneous volunteers asking to be subjects far in advance of the beginning of an experiment. Since we have used placebo and relatively unpleasant medications more frequently than drugs with desirable effects, we attribute our popularity to the fact that the men value the kind of contact they have with each other and with the staff. It seems to some to be an interesting way to learn about psychology. It is also true that we pay at the rate of one dollar per hour for the period from noon to 10:00 P.M.

While all this is going on, with the men producing their own data on the check lists and ratings of partners, the observers have made several kinds of records. The sound recorder has turned out a whole library of reels of tape, which we transcribed and tentatively analyzed only during the first year. From time to time, some observers have kept extensive impressionistic protocols. Some have recorded the Bales-Carter type of social interaction categories. Others have rated the men on scales roughly equivalent to the measures we were obtaining from the adjective check list. For some aspects of behavior, like drowsiness, social withdrawal, hostility, and task-involvement all these measures would tend to show the same trends due to drug. On aspects like elation, agreement was impossible. Agreement among such measures poses just as many interesting problems as do disagreements (cf., Nowlis[15]).

For purposes different from ours, Harrison Gough[5] set up the first long adjective check list I know about; he uses adjectives which apply to relatively permanent characteristics of the individual. He typically presents his analysis in the following way: he may take one hundred men who have been studied by ten observers at the University of California Institute for Personality Assessment and Research; on each of the test variables selected, he presents the adjectives most frequently checked by the staff as descriptive of the twenty-five highest scoring and twenty-five lowest scoring assessees on that variable. For example, in one study the twenty-five assessees scoring highest on the Strong Vocational

Interest Blank for the variable "Mortician" were described most frequently with the adjectives coarse, cynical, contented, confident, leisurely, and masculine. Those scoring highest on the variable "Psychologist," you will be pleased to learn, were given such adjectives as clear thinking, clever, complicated, imaginative, insightful, intelligent, etc. We have found this general method useful for a first over-all look at a drug effect. By contrast, our adjectives are selected as the verbal responses descriptive of aspects of mood. We can then examine how each adjective changes with an experimental treatment in any number of subjects and select those which give maximum discrimination between the experimental treatment and a control treatment.

Dramamine usually produces a definite increase in the checking of such words as tired, drowsy, detached, sluggish, disinterested, dull, lazy, retiring, withdrawn; and a definite decrease in the checking of such words as businesslike, genial, industrious, talkative, cheerful, energetic, etc. Partners' ratings and observers' ratings and protocols strongly tend to confirm such a picture.

An amphetamine most often increases the checking of such words as businesslike, talkative, capable, enterprising, independent, jittery; and decreases such words as lazy, languid, and nonchalant. An amphetamine plus seconal, in small dosage, may increase such words as generous, cheerful, industrious, expansive, expressive, talkative, lighthearted. In higher dosage the checking of assertive, confident, decisive, fearless, forceful, masterful, and uninhibited usually increases.

All is not so simple. At first we used the same drug for all four men. In those sessions, seconal, when compared with placebo, increased the checking of such words as expansive, forceful, courageous, daring, elated, and impulsive. In our first statistical analysis we were confronted with the stubborn fact that when the same drug is given to all four men in a group, the N that has to be entered into the analysis is one, not four. This increases the cost of an already expensive experiment by a considerable factor. But it cannot be denied that the effects of these drugs may be and often are quite contagious. Our first attempted solution was to run groups in which each man had a different drug during the same session, such as one on seconal, one on amphetamine, one on dramamine, and one on placebo. Now what does seconal do? Cooped up with, say, the egotistical amphetamine partner, the withdrawn dramamine partner who doesn't give a damn, and the slightly bored lactose man, the seconal subject reports that he is distractable, dizzy, drifting, glum, defiant, languid, sluggish, discouraged, dull, gloomy, lazy, and slow! This is not the report of mood we got when all four men were on seconal. It appears that the moods of the partners do definitely influence the effect of seconal. Furthermore, this influence, which is sometimes a relatively simple matter of contagion, may also involve much more indirect, conflictual social processes.

Last year we faced this problem directly in one four-week experiment. We selected two drugs we understood fairly well, dramamine and seconal, and predicted that the former would be less influenced by mood of partner than would the latter. In his own research at Rochester, William Haythorn [8] had worked out an ingenious schedule whereby from a pool of sixteen men each man over the course of five four-hour sessions would never work with the same partner more than once. We established two such pools of sixteen men each. In one pool, each man had one session when he was the only subject on dramamine, while the three others were on seconal; he had two sessions when he and two partners had dramamine and the fourth had seconal; in the fourth session he was on seconal as a stimulus partner for the other men on dramamine. This schedule permits us to compare the dramamine effect when the subject is grouped with three seconal partners, with the dramamine effect when he is in a group predominantly on dramamine. For the other pool we developed a similar schedule to compare the effect of seconal in the presence of partners who were predominantly on the same or different drug.

Three main instruments were used: (1) a long adjective check list administered at the start and finish of the three-hour session; (2) a short adjective check list for self-report after each of the three tasks in the pre-drug and in the post-drug periods; (3) the same short adjective check list filled out independently by two observers (Helen Nowlis and Jean Cameron) who had been taking protocols with the definite aim of discovering those specific behavioral changes which seemed crucial to them, after thousands of hours of experience, in the discrimination of medicated from nonmedicated behavior. Each observer filled out a check list for each subject as she predicted he would fill it out at the same time.

In scoring the long adjective check list, we used the

eighteen clusters of adjectives which we had derived empirically from the check lists of one hundred men in standard, nonmedicated situations. The short adjective check list consisted of an almost synonymous pair of words from each cluster and seven other pairs of words representing aspects of mood we felt had not emerged from the standard situations. Until we know all there is to know about mood, users of the adjective check list should not hesitate to add words selected for specific purposes.

The analysis of the data involved 136 different analyses of variance. First, to put the observers' over-all records in perspective, we find they correctly predicted the direction of change of mood in eighteen of the twenty-five clusters under dramamine and in twenty-three of the twenty-five under seconal. Painstaking and experienced as they are, they admit that they still cannot spell out to their own satisfaction all the cues they base their ratings on. They are still working on this important problem. The statistical analysis indicates that each observer did far better with some subjects than with others and better on some clusters than on others. Moreover, the two observers differed with respect to which subjects or clusters let her perform with maximum skill and insight.

As indicated both by observers and by self-report on the ACL, dramamine in the over-all analysis produced its usual effect of decreasing the scores in the clusters of active words and increasing scores in the clusters of sleepy and inactive words. Seconal produced its usual effect of increasing control and elation words, such as mischievous, original, willful, cheerful; but, like dramamine, it decreased scores in the active and industrious clusters.

The main hypothesis, that seconal is more influenced by mood of partner than is dramamine, received strong support. The contribution of the Group x Drug interaction term to the total variance is our test of whether or not the effect of the drug differed according to the kind of drug the subject's partners were on. GxD interaction was significantly large in two of the twenty-five clusters under dramamine and in eight of the twenty-five under seconal. To put it another way, the GxD interaction term was significantly large in 5 per cent of the sixty-eight analyses of dramamine and in 19 per cent of the sixty-eight analyses of variance involving seconal.

A subject on dramamine in a predominantly seconal group checks less frequently words in the disturbed and jittery clusters than when he is in a group which is predominantly on dramamine.

The GxD interactions in the seconal analysis reveal a very interesting effect. When the lone man on the seconal is grouped with three men on dramamine he reports that he is more industrious, careful, vigorous, boastful, jittery, and defiant and less drowsy, leisurely, and intoxicated than when he has two other partners on seconal. Three sluggish dramamine partners seem to sober him, alert him, and annoy and frustrate him. He reports a more positive mood when others are also on seconal.

Significant main effects due to task and to individual differences among the subjects were found in 11 per cent and in 45 per cent of the analyses, respectively.

These factors significantly interacted with drug effects in 13 per cent and 42 per cent of the analyses, respectively. That nature of the task influences drug effect is not surprising and suggests the importance of limiting any results to the specific task used in an experiment on drugs. Everyone expects, of course, to find individual differences in drug effects. Since we have not had more than thirty-two men in any one experiment, our samples have been too small to make a satisfactory search for the personality variables related to drug effects. We have, nevertheless, examined scores from many personality tests to help understand these individual differences. No personality test has yet helped us understand individual differences in either drug effect or social behavior in group situations. This is just another example of the general finding in social psychology[4] that prediction of behavior in experimental social groups is not yet possible on the basis of any of the well-known personality tests.

The many statistical analyses we have run, supplemented by our best judgment of factors that do not get into the analyses, suggest that the effects of behavior-modifying drugs in moderate dosage are tied down to specific individuals, in specific situations, performing specific tasks. These factors not only differ in hundreds of ways, they also interact with each other. Should the psychologist then decide to test this or that drug, in this or that dosage, in all kinds of people, in all kinds of social settings, doing a great variety of tasks? Such a program may be needlessly futile, since the laws by which individual, situation, and task interact have not yet been discovered.

To avoid the possibility of an ever narrowing focus, I suggest that the psychologist interested in drugs also continue to develop other research interests which seem important to him with the knowledge that drugs may at sometime or other assist him in the control or systematic variation of important factors in his research problem.

THE CONCEPT OF MOOD

We have in our drug work abundant evidence that the words in the adjective check list change in significant ways with experimental operations. Each operation produces a particular pattern of change. Moreover, the words change together in ways which produce interesting clusters. But these empirical clusters are not satisfactory because they are not sufficiently transituational; they are not yet useful in the search for general laws. In this section I am going (1) to attempt to define mood; (2) to set forth four tentative hypotheses about the dimensions of mood; and (3) describe a first step in testing these hypotheses.

In offering a definition of the concept of mood, I do not intend to cover the whole field of affect, feeling, and emotion. We want to set up, with objective definitions, a beachhead for limited research in this area. In what immediately follows, our debt to Magda Arnold,[1] Gustav Bergmann,[2] Brown and Farber,[3] Donald Lindsley,[12] Harold Schlosberg,[17] and B. F. Skinner[18] is obvious even though they will undoubtedly and justifiably repudiate us.

Mood (i.v.) as intervening variable is a hypothetical state which is a source of information (or discriminative stimuli) to the organism about the current functioning characteristics of the organism. Organism here refers to the *psychological* organism, not to a physiological or even psychophysiological organism. Eventually we would hope to encompass the latter concept. At present, we are concerned only with behavior, the operations which change or control behavior, and the intervening variables which may assist in an efficient search for these relationships. So for organism you may substitute, according to your preference, the words "person," "individual," or "self." Conscious mood (c.m.), also referred to here as perception of mood (c.m.), is the perceptual and cognitive response to this information. The term conscious experience or feeling may be substituted, if you prefer, for perceptual and cognitive response.

Mood (i.v.) may have a direct effect on the probabilities of certain responses in certain situations, as in expressive behavior and in action. Here it is like Skinner's[18] concept of predisposition, a state which directly changes the probabilites of certain acts. But mood (i.v.) has other effects which might be ignored if only the direct change in probability of certain overt acts is considered.

We assume that mood (i.v.) has a cue function when we define conscious mood (c.m.) as the response to cues supplied by the hypothetical mood state (i.v.). We may also make the gratuitous assumption that these cues, which supply information about the current functioning of the total organism, are involved in the monitoring and regulation of complex behavior.

Human organisms learn to label or respond verbally

to their conscious mood and to the discriminative stimuli supplied by mood (i.v.) with literally thousands of adjectives and descriptive phrases. The availability of these verbal responses in the form of adjectives gives us our present best index of the change in mood following experimental operations. We are painfully aware of the many factors which may interfere with accurate report of conscious mood; however, by studying them while manipulating mood through wide variations in many subjects, we hope to learn how to take these interfering factors into account.

The whole process of socialization of mood, of learning to inhibit, control, and modify mood, of using reports of mood in manipulating the social behavior of others, and of falsifying the report of it in certain situations has yet to be examined in research studies.

It is quite possible that mood (i.v.) also influences behavior indirectly by way of these verbal or mediating responses. For example, an individual who becomes tired in an unusual place at an unusual time will probably arrive at a resting place more quickly as a result of his self-report of fatigue. Spontaneous verbal responses of this sort might lead the individual to deliberate tests of just how he *is* functioning at the time.

Mood (i.v. or c.m.) is usually regarded as a more or less persistent state. A useful but not perfect discrimination between emotion (i.v.) and mood (i.v.) or between emotional response (conscious emotion) and conscious mood (c.m.) is that emotion is of short duration, mood is persistent. Furthermore, we suggest that emotional responses form one of the three general classes of antecedents of mood change (i.v.)

It is commonly believed that a brief, intense emotional response may change and set mood for some time. This may be a very useful idea. Furthermore, the functional association between emotion and mood is so close that the perceptual responses to emotion (i.v.) and to the resultant mood (i.v.) have many identical characteristics. We suggest that when emotion and mood are components in the same behavior sequence, emotional response is the onset and mood is the subsequent steady state. For analogy, we may recall that the onset symptoms of a drug are often similar to but easily discriminable from the symptoms of the subsequent steady state. The initial emotional response which sets the mood may be more intense and have an explosive flurry of action, very difficult to observe objectively or subjectively; by contrast, mood may often be relatively less intense, have less definite influence on behavior, but be more available for inspection and report by the subject and by the observer. By shifting our research focus from emotion to mood, we concentrate on the steady state that can be observed with some reliability and ignore in the present enterprise the rapid, complex, and important onset.

But we cannot ignore emotion entirely, even at this early stage of research, since it is one of the three classes of mood determinants. Such antecedents of emotion as deprivation, pain, frustration, restraint, conflict, sexual stimulation, success, and reward may indirectly influence mood by way of the emotional response. Furthermore, the originally neutral stimuli which through conditioning have acquired the capacity to evoke the emotional response also indirectly influence mood.

These conditioned stimuli include internal as well as external events, such as words, symbols, thoughts, ideas, images, perceptions, and drive stimuli of low intensity.

Now, in addition to the emotional response, there seem to be two other classes of factors which influence mood (i.v.). Here the possible role of emotional response is obscure; it may be absent. A survey of the literature indicates that moods have been found to be associated with: (1) operations which bring about persistent intra-organic processes and events such as metabolic and physiological changes, excess or foreign chemicals in the tissue, illness, shock, postoperative states, fatigue, brain injury, etc.; and (2) persistent environmental stimulation or deprivation, such as prolonged music, odors, visual stimulation, stress, or absence from home or of a loved one. How these two classes of antecedents influence mood is not known. We specify them here because they are in the pool of operations which influence a basic dependent variable, the verbal report of mood.

Gradual shifts in conscious mood due to persistent environmental stimulation may acquire an incentive value, a token reward or punishment value. The individual learns to seek out or arrange external or internal environmental situations which induce and sustain certain moods and to avoid those which induce certain other moods. A general theory of mood may also postulate that certain mood shifts, especially in hedonic tone, have a primary reinforcement function.

On the basis of our search for categories of mood-induced responses of general significance, I am tentatively postulating four bipolar dimensions of conscious mood (c.m.): level of activation; level of control; social orientation; and hedonic tone. Some, and perhaps all of these, are already in the literature.

Each of these postulated dimensions corresponds to a class of perceptions, having their basic source in mood (i.v.), of a general characteristic of the current functioning of the psychological organism. By assuming bipolarity we make the prior assumption that each dimension has a neutral point at which the individual does not know how to label his mood. This may be due, as suggested before, to the unavailability of discriminative stimuli at this point or due to the related fact that it has not been necessary for the individual to learn to discriminate and report this mood, perhaps because this mood state is of concern to no one in his culture and is ignored. Deviations from this neutral point in the two different directions bring about two qualitatively different perceptions of mood (c.m.). The greater the deviation from the neutral point, the more intense is the conscious mood (c.m.).

Level of activation refers to that aspect of mood in which there is perception of readiness for moving, acting, responding, working, thinking, paying attention, talking, solving problems, etc; in the negative pole there is perception of readiness not to move, act, etc., and readiness to rest or to sleep. This dimension is somewhat analogous to Donald Lindsley's[12] concept of activation level, to Harold Schlosberg's[17] similar dimension, derived from the study of facial expressions, and to Osgood's activity factor,[16] derived from factor analyses of meaning. A few of the positive adjectives tentatively assigned to this dimension are active, alert, attentive, industrious, and lively. Examples of negative adjectives are slow, sluggish, and sleepy.

Level of control refers to that aspect of mood in which there is perception of the degree to which internal and external events are, have been, or will be under control, or the degree to which they are out of control. This may be a new dimension. It is slightly similar to the traditional organized-disorganized dichotomy. Examples of positive adjectives tentatively assigned to this dimension are confident, effective, resourceful, assured, optimistic, secure, brave, and proud. Negative examples include confused, dubious, indecisive, helpless, apprehensive, hesitant, remorseful, and sorry. We are tentatively putting our clusters of guilt and apprehension adjectives under the negative pole of this dimension since helplessness is an important component of anxiety; as for guilt and shame, the self-inflicted or anticipated punishment seems beyond the control of the individual. We may find that these clusters may fall elsewhere, as in the hedonic tone dimension.

Social orientation refers to that aspect of mood in which there is perception of readiness to have mutually comforting interaction with other persons or, readiness to hurt, reject, or ignore others. This is similar to but different from dependency-aggression, love-hate. Since we are trying to explore the usefulness of the concept of mood, we have chosen the term social orientation to avoid the many implications of these other terms. Attraction-rejection might do as well.

Tentative examples of positive adjectives include trustful, compliant, generous, kindly, affectionate, and warmhearted. Negative examples include aloof, suspicious, belligerent, sarcastic, angry, and annoyed.

Hedonic tone refers to that aspect of mood in which there is perception of pleasantness or unpleasantness. It is the classical dimension in the description of mood. Tentative examples of positive adjectives include cheerful, playful, amused, delighted, and elated. Negative examples include blue, downhearted, disturbed, miserable.

What the specific antecedents of change in each of these postulated dimensions are, and what the other behavioral accompaniments of such change are, remain to be seen. We have some notions about this, but I mention the problem here only to note in passing that the dimensions will be significant only if such relations are established.

We are probably warranted in assuming some degree of independence among these dimensions since our previous work suggests that conscious moods may be found which represent combinations of any two poles of any two dimensions.

Functionally, the four aspects of mood may interact in several loci. First, there may be interaction at the intervening variable level. Second, the perceptual and verbal responses to one aspect of mood change may result in a change in another aspect. For example, increase in activation level of an individual who has been consistently rewarded for behavior resulting from high level of activation may lead to increase in hedonic tone. Third, the perception of consistency or of discrepancy between conscious mood, as an indicator of present functioning characteristics of the organism, and the current demands of the environment on the organism may give rise to mood change. The individual whose mood is a perception of readiness to work and who finds no work to do may soon have a decrease in hedonic level. Similarly, a person in the mood to rest who has to work may soon be in a bad mood.

Some of you may still ask why we even consider different categories or dimensions of mood. The answer is, as David McClelland put it last year, that we are inextricably involved in the analysis of some of the myriad verbal responses which describe mental content; and in such an analysis one must find categories which are "meaningful; they must be related to theory; they must be transituational—i.e., they must be applicable to more situations than the one to which they are first applied. It takes inspiration or luck or hard work or something to discover such a category; . . . the only concrete suggestion I have . . . is to choose those categories which show significant shifts as a result of experimental operations."[13] To repeat, we have abundant evidence that the responses to the adjectives on our check list vary with many different experimental operations. Each operation produces a particular pattern of change. But the empirical clusters which we now use to score mood change are not yet satisfactory because they are not sufficiently transituational; they are not easily related to the search for general laws. The present postulated dimensions may do better. To test the present hypotheses we have initiated a study of the verbal responses to one hundred adjectives in five hundred men subjected to six different experimental operations designed to change mood. With the help of the IBM 650 soon to be available at the University of

Rochester, we will do a factor analysis of the responses in the first pre-experimental check list and on each of the six postexperimental lists. If the factors which emerge in all situations correspond to our postulated dimensions, we will know they are transituational. Analysis of pre-post differences will indicate how factor scores change with experimental operations. We should then have sufficient knowledge to search for the relations between these dimensions and their behavioral antecedents and consequents in fairly general terms. Russell Green has worked out the statistical design of this project. Burton Andreas, Bernard Harleston, and Sheldon Alexander will collaborate. The project is sponsored by the Group Psychology Branch of the Office of Naval Research.

COMMUNICATIONS AND MOOD

For reasons such as the foregoing, we became interested in a search for nonchemical manipulators of mood in much larger numbers of subjects than can be used in drug work. We did some work on habitability factors and boredom; Victor Laties[11] worked with sleep deprivation; Sheldon Alexander induced mood change in task-involved dyads by controlling the informational and affective content of the written messages which the partners sent to each other. Fortunately the Janis-Feshbach study came to my attention. These workers gave three different illustrated lectures to groups of high school students. The lectures differed from each other in the vividness and completeness of detail with which pathological dental conditions were presented. They were designed to represent three levels of fear appeal. They report that 74 per cent of the subjects who heard the high fear appeal admitted that they were disturbed during the lecture while only 48 per cent of the subjects in the low fear group reported that they were disturbed. Subjects in the high fear group were less persuaded to accept the recommended dental habits than were subjects in the low fear group. The study provides us with a model in which (1) a readily controlled determinant of mood (the communication with its emotional detail and vivid illustrations) changes (2) verbal report of mood ("emotional disturbance") and (3) another independently defined behavioral index, report of opinion change, in (4) very large numbers of subjects in a short time. The research possibilities with this model and its attendant theory are tremendous, as Janis and Feshbach undoubtedly realized when they established it.

Don P. Haefner,[6] in our social psychology laboratory, has worked out an important extension of the Janis and Feshbach findings. He has developed and taped four fifteen-minute communications in an area of much greater ego involvement than dental hygiene, namely, the history and control of thermonuclear weapons. Two of these tapes emphasize fear by describing the damage to Rochester if the bomb fell in Buffalo. One of the tapes (high fear) contains many more vivid references to personal injury and suffering than does the other (low fear); but both contain the same basic information. The other two experimental tapes emphasize guilt by describing the damage we have inadvertently brought to innocent victims. As in the case of fear, one of these (high guilt) emphasizes vivid details, while the other is more objective (low guilt). A fifth, or control tape, discusses the United Nations with no reference to atomic weapons. The final part of each experimental message has a standard recommendation that international agreements be worked out for the temporary cessation of H-bomb tests. Three weeks after an initial opinion survey the tapes were played to five groups of sixty-seven men each, on a single evening. Each group heard one tape. An analysis of the adjective check lists which were administered just before and after the experimental message, indicates that each message produced highly significant increases in the checking of words specifying descriptive mood for which it had been designed. Moreover, the Janis-Feshbach hypothesis was supported in both the fear and guilt areas; the subjects who heard a high-level tape accepted the recommendation less readily than did those hearing a low-level tape.

With the cooperation of Haefner, we gathered from his subjects extra data which we have been examining in the following ways. We have found that each tape also produced a special pattern of associated mood responses, as reported on the adjective check list. First, *in comparison with the men who had just heard the control tape,* the men who had just heard any one of the four experimental tapes reported they were significantly more attentive and less bored, sleepy, and washed out; they also reported they were significantly less humorous and witty. Finally, they reported they were significantly more anxious, apprehensive, and cautious; more blue, downhearted, and sad; and more excited, shocked, and uneasy.

When we compare reports of the men who had just heard the fear tapes with those who had just heard the guilt tapes, the check lists of the subjects in the fear groups indicated that they were significantly more apprehensive, disturbed, and uneasy; more attentive and serious; and more reserved. The men who had just heard the guilt tapes, in contrast to the men in the fear groups, reported they were more active, talkative, and uninhibited; more calm and confident; more boastful and elated; more detached and indifferent; more belligerent and sarcastic; as well as more repentant and sorry. Whereas the fear tapes led to a mood which was reported as quiet and attentive without a decrease in positive social orientation, the guilt tapes led to an explosive type of mood, with increase in negative social orientation and a conflict between control and lack of control.

When we compare the two high-level tapes with the two low-level, we find that the men who had just heard the former checked significantly more frequently such words as blue, downhearted, and unhappy; apprehensive, jittery, shocked, and uneasy; sorry and suspicious.

These results indicate that emotional communications can induce for short periods complex moods which are reported as definitely and precisely as anything we obtained with medication. Determination of the intricate relationships between the content of such communications and the resultant mood is an obvious next step; to progress toward this problem we have set up the four hypotheses about the dimensions of mood, which we are now checking.

Content of the message alone is not the only determinant of mood. Our analysis of the records of the 268 men in the experimental groups shows that the men who were originally in favor of the recommended opinion reported a different change in mood after hearing the tape than did the men originally against the opinion. Those originally in favor showed a significantly greater increase in checking words in the disturbed and apprehensive clusters than did those originally opposed. Furthermore, those in favor of the recommended opinion *after* hearing the tape more frequently checked the words doubtful and unsure, and the words confident and egotistic less frequently than did those who finally rejected the opinion.

As our work in this area of communication, persuasion, and mood continues we shall be continually on the alert for any discovery by our colleagues of drugs which, with a minimum of side effects, produce effects which include a change in such limited aspects of mood as anxiety, hostility, self-confidence, positive social orientation, hesitancy and uncertainty, and activity level. If by that time we will have established, in large numbers of subjects, certain fairly dependable relationships between mood and its nonchemical antecedents and consequents, the drug will be of the greatest help to us, and we, in turn, shall be able to evaluate with efficiency one aspect of its effects.

BIBLIOGRAPHY

1. Arnold, Magda. The Status of Emotion in Contemporary Psychology. In Robach, A. A. (ed.). *Present Day Psychology*. New York: Philosophical Library, 1955.
2. Bergmann, Gustav. Theoretical psychology. *Ann. Rev. Psychol.*, 1953, 4: 435-58.

3. Brown, J. S., and Farber, I. E. Emotions conceptualized as intervening variables—with suggestions toward a theory of frustration. *Psychol. Bull.*, 1951, 48: 465-95.

4. Festinger, Leon. Social psychology and group processes. *Ann. Rev. Psychol.*, 1955, 6: 187-216.

5. Gough, H., McKee, M. G., and Yandell, R. J. *Adjective Check List Analyses of a Number of Selected Psychometric and Assessment Variables*. Berkley, Calif.: Institute of Personality Assessment and Research, 1953.

6. Haefner, Don P. "Some Effects of Guilt-arousing and Fear-arousing Persuasive Communications on Opinion Change." Unpublished Ph.D. thesis, University of Rochester, 1956.

7. Harway, V. T., Lanzetta, J. T., Nowlis, H. H., Nowlis, V., and Wendt, G. R. Chemical Influences on Behavior: II. Development of methods and preliminary results on the effects of some drugs on emotional and social behavior. (Technical Report, Project ONR 144-060) 1953.

8. Haythorn, William. The influence of individual members on the characteristics of small groups. *J. Abnorm. Soc. Psychol.*, 1953, 48: 276-84.

9. Hovland, C. I., Janis, I. L., and Kelley, H. H. *Communication and Persuasion*. New Haven: Yale University Press, 1953.

10. Janis, I. L., and Feshbach, S. Effects of fear-arousing communication. *J. Abnorm. Soc. Psychol.*, 1953, 48: 78-92.

11. Laties, Victor. "The Modification of Affective Response, Social Behavior and Group Performance by Sleep Deprivation and Medication." Unpublished Ph.D. thesis, University of Rochester, 1954.

12. Lindsley, Donald. Emotion. In Stevens, S. S. (ed.). *Handbook of Experimental Psychology*. New York: John Wiley & Sons, Inc., 1951.

13. McClelland, D. The psychology of mental content reconsidered. *Psychol. Rev.*, 1955, 62: 297-302.

14. Nowlis, H. H., Nowlis, V., Riesen, A. H., and Wendt, G. R. Chemical influences on behavior. III. The effects of dramamine and scopolamine on emotional and social behavior with comparison data on the effects of other drugs. (Technical Report, Project ONR 144-060) 1953.

15. Nowlis, V. The development and modification of motivational systems in personality. In Brown, J. S., *et al. Current Theory and*

Research in Motivation: A Symposium. Lincoln, Nebraska: University of Nebraska Press, 1953.

16. Osgood, C. E., and Suci, G. J. Factor analysis of meaning. *Psychol. Rev.,* 1955, 50: 325-38.
17. Schlosberg, Harold. Three dimensions of emotion. *Psychol. Rev.,* 1954, 61: 81-97.
18. Skinner, B. F. *Science and Human Behavior.* New York: Macmillan Co., 1953.
19. Solomon, Richard. Learning under curare. Colloquium given at the University of Rochester, January, 1956.

THE MEDIATION HYPOTHESIS IN THE ANALYSIS AND DESCRIPTION OF BEHAVIOR

CHARLES N. COFER

I should like to acknowledge the helpful comments and suggestions made as this paper was being prepared by Richard Gonzalez, David King, Thomas Sprecher, and Phillip Welsh.

IN an era in which emphasis in the psychological study of behavior on cognitive and integrative processes seems once again to be growing, it has seemed appropriate to examine the mediation hypothesis. This hypothesis, which, as far as I know, was named as such by Osgood,[17] has had, in a number of guises, a considerable history. Into this history I shall not enter but instead be content with the statement that, among the latter-day psychologists whose fealty to Hull and Guthrie and their intellectual ancestors remains strong, the mediation hypothesis is a white knight whose jousting is with such as expectancy, re-centering, direction, insight, and organization, the habiliments of which, I might add, are of the blackest black.

What are the functions of the mediation hypothesis, that is, why should a mediation process be postulated? The general answer, I think, is that sometimes behavior does not reflect direct stimulus-response or response-response association, i.e., a response may occur to a stimulus to which it has never been associated, or overt responses may occur in sequence without a prior history of frequent instances of such sequential linkage. In the first case the mediation hypothesis usually has the name of mediated, acquired, or secondary generalization, and it is advanced to explain instances of stimulus equivalence. In the second case, it is advanced to explain sequences in responses, as in the case of free or controlled association, in which the particular sequence is unusual or difficult to understand, or, it may be suggested in cases, as in problem solving or concept formation, in which a novel combination of ideas or experiences leads to a solution. Similar usages were made by Hull[8] in his analyses of "foresight," "purpose," and related notions; his concept was the "pure stimulus act," which, so far as I can see, is another name for the mediation hypothesis (see also Dollard and Miller[5]).

In the discussion which follows, I should like to illustrate the application of the mediation notion to several problem areas, indicating its presumed advantages as compared with other notions. Then I shall formulate the hypothesis in a more formal vein and conclude with a discussion of its role in the analysis of verbal behavior.

APPLICATIONS OF THE MEDIATION HYPOTHESIS

In problem solving a critical element seems to be that the subject must perceive aspects of the situation and respond to them in ways which are relevant to the solution which is required, i.e., there must be a selective factor in the responses which are elicited or which are emitted as he works on the problem. Thus, if he is required to solve the problem of tying together two strings which are suspended from the ceiling but which are not long enough for him to reach them both at the same time from a standing position it is necessary that he perceive those characteristics of the materials at hand which are relevant to the various solutions which are possible. As Maier[12] carried out experiments with this problem, there was a pair of pliers present on a table. Maier intended that the subject should perceive that if one string were set in motion, like a pendulum, the problem could be solved by grasping one string and catching the other as it swings over to the subject. The pair of pliers was to be attached to one string, thereby weighting it and permitting it to swing in a suitable fashion. For the subject to reach this solution it would seem necessary for him *(a)* to get the notion of a swinging string, *(b)* to recognize that a weighted string would swing more widely and more directionally than an unweighted string, and *(c)* to react to the pliers as a weight.

Now if the subject could make some sort of response in this situation which would amount to the notion of swinging strings then the likelihood would be that he would at once look for some heavy object to tie to a string and then set the string in motion. In this instance the notion of swinging strings is a mediating response which is associated, presumably, with further responses having to do with using weights and setting the string in motion. Maier was able to induce solutions of this sort by brushing against a string, setting it in motion. This "hint" would frequently lead to pendulum or swinging solutions, and Maier suggested the concept of *direction* as necessary to the occurrence of such "productive" solutions. But direction is a rather vague and general notion, which does not readily suggest operations whereby the phenomenon can be further described or studied. As a matter of fact Maier has suggested that accidental events (such as the apparently accidental brushing of the string) are often required for the subject to reach an unusual or productive solution.

The advantages of the mediation hypothesis are, I think, in this case that the mediating response can be a relatively specific, identifiable process; further, it can be studied. For example, if its likelihood of occurrence can be changed, by operations independent of the actual problem-solving situation, then there should be changes in the frequency with which the solution it mediates occurs. Similarly, if the instrumental responses to which the mediating response gives rise can be modified, then, too, effects on problem solution can be observed. So there are at least two points at which inquiry can be directed, from a mediation hypothesis viewpoint, certainly an advantage over what is provided by the notion of direction.

It should be clear from the foregoing example that the mediation process is one whose function is to provide for the directedness or selectivity which behavior often displays. It might be fair to describe it as a hypothetical account of some types of set, as well as of other concepts whose function is directional but whose mechanism is unspecified, like attitude, disposition, determining tendency, *Bewussteinslage,* etc. It seems clear to me that as the experimental psychologist increases the emphasis of his investigations on problems in which such processes as set are involved he will find the mediation hypothesis useful and that he will find it necessary to develop means of measuring or assessing the mediating tendencies which subjects bring with them to the experimental situation. A good example of what I mean is provided by some work on the learning and retention of meaningful material which some graduate assistants and I are carrying out under a contract with the Office of Naval Research. We have not solved the problems to which I have alluded, but a brief description of what is involved may point up the necessity for solutions before productive work can be carried out.

To anyone who has worked in the area of the learning and retention of meaningful material it is clear that processes go on which are hardly even suggested when nonsense materials or lists of discrete meaningful words are investigated. Even in the latter instances, of course, the literature does describe such procedures as grouping, rhythm, and association of nonsense materials with more meaningful or familiar words. These tendencies have been given relatively little significance in the study of learning. Recently, however, George Miller[15] has argued that the "channel capacity" of the human operator or his ability to perceive and retain discrete and unorganized elements of information is limited; he points to the limited "memory span" and to other performances of human subjects and suggests that at best such individuals can apprehend and retain around seven or eight or nine such discrete items. On its face this assertion seems ridiculous, and we should probably all agree that the memory span situation is atypical in the estimates it gives of human capacities of memory. Miller is quite aware of this, but he points out that perhaps the memory span is deficient not in the estimate it gives of "raw" memory ability, but rather in the opportunities it provides for organizing or coding processes to take place.

Perhaps I can make these points clearer by describing a brief experiment cited by Miller. Suppose a subject is asked to listen to a single presentation of a random series of numbers made up of the digits 0 and 1. About the best he can do is to repeat back perhaps eight or nine of them accurately. Now suppose that the subject learns a coding system, so that, say, the letter A stands for the sequence 001, B for 010, C for 100, etc. We find that after this code is learned he can repeat accurately a much longer series than eight or nine digits, and if his code is fully enough developed and adequately learned he may be able to listen once to as many as forty randomly presented binary digits and repeat them without error. The point is that the coding system has enormously increased the subject's apparent memory ability.

Miller's argument strongly suggests that coding systems or organizing processes are fundamental to all memory performances beyond the memory span, and he would probably interpret the acquisition of a list of paired associates or of a list of items by the method of serial anticipation in terms of coding or organizing processes operative through the sequence of trials.

If Miller's interpretations are correct, and it must be obvious that I am much impressed by them, then it follows that coding and organizing processes are the major substance of the study of human learning. One might wonder if this is what Gestalt psychologists, like George Katona,[11] have been saying all along. I will say here only that I have an impression that Miller and the Gestalt psychologists are less in agreement than the foregoing discussion may suggest, but this impression, I should point out, is perhaps but a servant to my own deep-seated resistances to much of Gestalt psychology.

I bring these matters into this discussion because coding and organizing processes would seem to be obvious instances to which the operation and understanding provided by the mediation hypothesis could apply. As my associates and I have thought about the area of meaningful learning and retention we have attempted to think of coding and organizing factors as instances of mediational processes, and I should like to summarize our thinking here. We think we can identify three classes of such processes. I shall list these first, returning to each one for brief commentary later.

First, there are what we shall call coding processes, illustrated by the experiment with digits cited above as well as by Katona's numerous studies[11] and by Postman's recent work on retention of figures.[19] I would characterize coding processes as reflecting the explicit, *ad hoc* formulation of a principle or procedure, which permits efficient retention or reconstruction of the materials presented.

Second, I would suggest another class which I shall call ordering processes. These would include the use of grouping, rhythm, and mnemonic associations, as well as the influence of linguistic habits and linguistic structure, which, as I pointed out some years ago,[4] seem to operate importantly when subjects are required to learn connected discourse, like prose passages or stories. This class probably shows an automatic application by people to wide classes of learning situations, especially in verbal learning, and is probably not ordinarily explicitly verbalized or even perhaps verbalizable.

The third class would consist of the hypothesized processes relating attitudes and motivational or personality variables chiefly to changes introduced during recall. Bartlett's concept of the schema,[1] as well as motivated forgetting, would be included here. Such processes again are perhaps widely generalized and ordinarily unverbalized or unverbalizable. We may as well code this class as schematizing processes. I might say that it is not entirely clear to me to what extent schematizing processes are independent of ordering processes, the second class. It is probable that their influences are almost always confounded, at any rate.

To return to coding processes, it seems unlikely that the explicit formulation of a code for the purpose of recalling a particular series of verbal stimuli can usefully be classed as a mediating process; it would seem to be a set of responses developed as an instrumental means by which the situation can be mastered. But the notion or concept of coding might well be retained and occur to the subject on the next occasion in which he must learn a large number of items, even though the specific character of the items in no way resembles that of the first set of items coded. The notion of coding in this second case could legitimately be regarded as a mediating response or process, the stimulational consequences of which could lead to further symbolic manipulations which might lead to a code. It is quite possible, too, that elements of an already developed code might be transferred to a new and different situation, with further instrumental effects of this transfer. To the extent that the notion of coding or parts of a code automatically transfer as implicit responses which lead to further instrumental operations of coding, they have certainly become mediating responses.

As to ordering processes it is not clear to what extent mediational as opposed to directly applicable responses are involved. The human subjects we ordinarily use in learning and retention studies are individuals who are highly practiced in the art of learning, and they may transfer directly to new situations ordering processes, such as those involved in linguistic structure, which they have quite thoroughly overlearned. It may be, of course, that mediational responses would be necessary to circumvent the automatic transfer of ordering processes in a new learning situation in which the learning goal is incompatible with the effects of ordering processes. We are only beginning to explore this area. Last summer we had a number of subjects study and then reproduce over several time intervals the Bartlett story, *War of the Ghosts.* One of my assistants, Mr. David King, noted that the original story has an unusually low proportion of adjectives to verbs. Scoring the reproductions for the adjective-verb quotient, he found that the mean proportion of adjectives to verbs in the recalls was always greater than in the original story and that it tended to become even larger with subsequent recalls. We do not at present know what this finding means or what is its relation to accuracy in recall, and we are presently studying many more data collected from recalls of stories written specifically to vary in the adjective-verb ratio. Whether the increase in the AVQ represents the operation of a mediating process or simply the direct effects of the typical language habits and structure of our subjects remains to be seen. If it suggests the latter, then a mediating process might be required to overcome such habits in the interest of better recall. What this means is that language habits may be highly stable characteristics of subjects which are automatically transferred to or evoked by situations involving learning connected materials. If such language habits are incompatible with highly accurate or efficient recall of the material, then a response which would mediate reactions other than these stable language habits might be necessary to make satisfactory recall possible.

On the other hand, it may be that a mediating response is required in order that particular characteristics of style, at any rate, be selected for a particular writing or learning task. It seems likely that this is so, because it seems intuitively sound that one's style varies as he contemplates writing a short story or a scientific paper, or as he contemplates memorizing a story verbatim or for substance. Considerable research is needed on these points.

Mr. Richard Gonzalez, another assistant, has been studying the efficiency in recall of sentences which vary in meaningfulness but which are composed of words of equal Thorndike-Lorge frequency and which have the same form or structure. This study could be illustrated if one compared the retention of a proverb, which is rich in implications, with a closely similar sentence with relatively few implications. Preliminary data suggest that in retention the relatively unmeaningful sentence on the average is slightly superior or equivalent to the proverb-like sentence for short time intervals but that the superiority shifts in the longer retention intervals (two to seven days) to favor the proverb-like sentence. We decided to study these sentences in order to determine whether the stylistic or contextual features were the primary determiners of efficiency in recall, following a suggestion by Miller and Selfridge.[16] It seems that the superior delayed retention of the highly meaningful sentences will require a mediation interpretation if it is confirmed by further observations.

Schematizing processes are as little understood as ordering processes. You will perhaps recall that Bartlett emphasized the role of the schema in filtering what was studied so that in recall the materials reproduced would be more orderly, logical, conventional, and acceptable than they were in the original story. Schachtel[23] and Maslow[13, Chapter 14] have similarly called attention to such effects, and phenomena like motivated forgetting and better learning of material congruent with one's attitudes and beliefs may represent similar processes. We suspect that the mediation hypothesis will have great applicability here, although in this class the study of the mediating processes subjects bring to the task will have to be stressed. To date we have contented ourselves with some rather simple studies designed to get at the extent to which and the conditions under which schematizing processes occur. For example, we have completed all but the data analysis stage of a study in which the major variable investigated was the instructional set under which the Bartlett ghost story was learned. Perhaps instructions mediate reactions which cue off various responses making for more or less accuracy in recall. Another obvious variable which needs investigation is the degree of bizarreness or unconventionality which the original story contains; we need to know some of the limits to which schematizing processes are subject.

In summary of this field of meaningful learning and retention, it would seem that the mediation hypothesis ought to have fruitful implications for the exploration of an area, which, like problem solving, has been relatively neglected. Its promise, however, has not as yet been fully realized. It will force us, I think, to make specific hypotheses about processes which heretofore have either been largely ignored, like ordering processes, or have been treated in the vaguest of terms, like schematizing processes.

It is tempting to continue this discussion of problems to which the mediation hypothesis might be applied. For example, in perception, concept formation, and transposition phenomena in discriminative behavior it has interesting implications. In these areas the function of the hypothesis is chiefly that of mediating equivalence reactions, whereas in problem solving and meaningful learning, as I have discussed them, its function seems more that of mediating selection among and direction of responses. However, I think it is time now to deal with the hypothesis somewhat more formally and then to discuss some aspects of its utilization in verbal behavior.

THE MEDIATION HYPOTHESIS

The hypothesis rests on the observation that parts of a total response which is originally made to a stimulus or situation may on a subsequent occasion appear either in anticipation of the occurrence of the total response or may appear even though the circumstances for the full response never come about. Further, it is assumed that this fractional, anticipatory response has stimulational effects and that to these effects other responses, perhaps instrumental ones, can be associated. There is no essential reason, so far as I can see, to restrict the mediating process to fractional responses, but the functional significance of mediating responses is presumably enhanced, if, as Osgood[17, p. 397] observes, they require little effort, can become anticipatory in time, and are not much affected by competition with other responses. To the extent that they become fractional, mediating responses meet these criteria. That so much emphasis is placed on verbal responses by those who stress mediational processes is partly because verbal responses can often meet these criteria where other responses cannot. The stress on verbal responses also arises from the belief that much of human behavior is mediated, and verbal behavior, of course, is highly present in human beings. However, other kinds of mediating responses will probably be required in many of the situations to which the hypothesis may be applied.

Quite clearly the mediation hypothesis provides, for the experienced organism, a means for the transfer of learning from one situation to another. The problem here is to make the mediating response occur; once it occurs the responses to which its stimulus effects lead should follow automatically. The real difficulty with the mediating response is that it can be postulated even though it is covert and unverbalized; these properties make it difficult to identify and hard to define the types and dimensions of such responses. Care must be exercised to prevent its promiscuous use as an explanation in situations in which its occurrence cannot be reasonably inferred or demonstrated.

There are, however, a number of experiments in which mediating responses have been observed and demonstrated. These are in addition to the many studies in which fractional anticipatory goal reactions have been used to deduce or to account for aspects of maze behavior or of secondary reinforcement. Thus, the experiments by Shipley[24] and by Lumsdaine[6, pp. 230-32] provide an early demonstration in a conditioning situation. Shipley paired a light with a tap to the cheek, which elicited the wink response. Following this, the tap was paired with a shock to the finger, eliciting finger retraction. Then the light, which had never been paired with finger retraction, was found to elicit it. Lumsdaine's records show, in some instances at least, that the wink response occurred between the light and the finger retraction on the test trials, so presumably the wink mediated the occurrence of the finger movement when the light was presented. This experiment should be repeated with electrical recording of muscle potentials; one would expect that there would be no finger response to the light unless there were some evidence of muscular activity related to the wink. Wickens and Briggs[25] have recently demonstrated that a mediating response may play a significant role in sensory preconditioning.

In an experiment by May[14] rats were taught to jump a hurdle to escape shock. Later, one group of animals was kept in an enclosure while a buzzer was paired with shock; in another enclosed group the buzzer and the shock were presented but not in association. On later occasions outside the enclosure a larger proportion of the first group jumped the hurdle to the buzzer (no shock being present) than of the second group. Here, presumably, the response to shock mediated the transfer of the jumping response to the buzzer.

Birge's extensive investigation[2] showed that children would transfer a manipulative response learned from one box to another box which had the same name. The degree of this transfer was increased if the naming response was made aloud during the transfer test and during the stage of learning the manipulation response. Jeffrey[9] has confirmed essentially Birge's results and also has shown transfer based upon a nonverbal mediating response. Russell and Storms[22] recently have offered convincing evidence of mediation processes in human learning. They paired nonsense syllables with words. After these pairs were learned, the nonsense syllables were paired with additional words. Some of these words were highly frequent associates of other words (never used in the experiment) which in turn were highly frequent associates of the first words to be paired with the nonsense syllables. Learning was facilitated for these words which had associative and presumably mediating links with the words in the first pairs. Yarczower[26] has confirmed these results.

These studies clearly support some of the essential features of the mediation hypothesis, but we clearly need many more direct studies of the mediation process. We certainly need a more adequate taxonomy of mediating responses than we have at present, and we need extensive investigations of the relationships between the discriminative and symbolic capacities of organisms and their mediating abilities. And we need a great deal more of critical and analytic thinking concerning the definition, characteristics, and identification of mediating processes. The evident absence of rigor in what I have said cannot be attributed to the fact that this paper has been prepared for a general audience.

THE MEDIATION HYPOTHESIS AND VERBAL BEHAVIOR

I had originally intended to devote my entire time to this particular topic. But the study of verbal behavior is still a rather special one and besides the mediation hypothesis has standing, as I have tried to show, independently of verbal behavior. There are, I think, at least two orientations to the study of verbal behavior. One conceives verbal behavior as important largely in terms of its mediational functions so far as other behavior or behavioral outcomes are concerned.

The section on the higher mental processes in Dollard and Miller's book[5] illustrates this approach. The other orientation looks at verbal behavior in its own right as a legitimate subject of inquiry. Obviously, the two approaches have much in common, but I think they lead to somewhat different emphases. Insofar as the mediating processes involved in problem solving and meaningful learning, for example, are verbal they would illustrate the first orientation, and it is obvious that the greater our knowledge about verbal behavior itself the greater is our ability to understand its role in mediating other behaviors.

Mediational processes can be and are being studied in various ways within the verbal behavior area itself. It is, I think, clear that a major impetus was given to emphasis on the mediation hypothesis by the studies on semantic generalization in conditioned responses by Razran,[20] Riess,[21] and others. In current research, perhaps four illustrations will suffice to indicate the directions in which research on verbal behavior are going, which are of interest to the psychologist.

One of these is the work of Bousfield and his associates.[3] It has been commonly observed for many years that, in free association, clusters of apparently related responses seem to occur. Bousfield has invented a technique whereby these tendencies may be studied. One simply makes up a list of *n* words which fall into specifiable categories. For example, one might select ten vegetables, ten animals, ten cities, and ten occupations, making a total of forty words. The words are then read to subjects in a randomized order, and the subject is asked to recall as many as he can. One can then study the recalls to observe the occurrence of clusters of words from the same group; clusters are of course imposed by the subject on the original randomized sequence. Clustering occurs quite widely, and Bousfield has been studying conditions of which clustering is a function. He finds clustering to be related to the number of readings of the original list, the Thorndike-Lorge familiarity of the words, the number of categories from which words are drawn, and so on. It is quite likely, I think, that clustering involves mediating processes, and Bousfield would no doubt agree, and that further work with these methods may lend a great deal of light to the understanding and definition of mediating and organizing processes. Bousfield himself is partial to organizing factors conceived in Hebb's terms.

Another emphasis is represented by the work of Jenkins and Russell.[10, 22] Rather than stressing meaning, as Bousfield and Osgood have done, they have stressed direct associative connections, as shown in Kent-Rosanoff associative frequency tables. I should add that it can be argued whether mediating processes (meaning) are or are not involved in some or all of the associations to verbal stimuli. Certainly, these investigators have shown mediational effects, as I have already indicated in alluding to the Russell-Storms study, and they have shown that clustering will occur in a Bousfield situation when words are used in the original randomized list which have known associative frequency relationships to one another. Selecting their materials from words with known associative frequency relationships, Jenkins and Russell have not emphasized mediational processes, except in the learning experiment of Russell and Storms. I think their work will force a better and more rigorous formulation of the mediation hypothesis and lead to tests which will clearly delineate its role in verbal behavior.

Some of their findings offer highly interesting problems. In one study, for example, they presented on a sheet a number of Kent-Rosanoff stimulus words and in the response column of the sheet the initial letter of and a suitable number of spaces for response words of known frequency of occurrence to these stimuli. Under these conditions an enormous increase in the frequency of these response words was observed. While the partial response structure was the operational variable which is associated with this effect, one wonders if it could work independently of some mediating process in a situation of this kind. Further research will be necessary to decide this point. In another study, a fourteen-word list was read once to some subjects. Then a free association test was given, among which were fourteen stimuli to which the fourteen previously read words were known to be low frequency responses. Again, there was a large increase in the frequencies with which these fourteen response words were given to the appropriate stimuli in this free association test. This phenomenon they have called recency. I might prefer to call it priming of mediating processes, and eventually intend to devote some time to study of this phenomenon, because I think it has great implications for problems of response availability in areas ranging from perception to problem solving.

Another current research approach is represented

by Osgood's development[17, 18] of the semantic differential, a technique which so far seems to get at connotative meaning. He has asked subjects to rate a variety of concepts on a number of bipolar scales anchored by adjectives, e.g., happy and sad. Factor analysis of the resulting intercorrelations of the ratings has revealed three dimensions of judgment: an evaluative, a potency, and an activity dimension. This procedure and its results to date go a long way toward the solution of dimensional questions with regard to verbal mediational processes, although as Osgood recognizes, denotative meanings have not yet been tapped in his studies. Time does not permit a further treatment of his extensive program, which in both theoretical and empirical investigation probably has no peer among students of language and the mediation hypothesis.

Lastly, I should like to refer again to the work of G. A. Miller, whose study with Selfridge[16] recognizes and offers an important methodological approach to the problem of context (see also, Howes and Osgood[7]). In their study Miller and Selfridge showed that contextual dependencies or constraints were highly significant factors in the retention of texts composed of meaningful English words. I do not have time to describe their technique for varying contextual dependencies within a text, but I think it is possible that the context factors may heavily involve mediating processes in ways which simply cannot be studied except by methods of the type they used.

In summary, I have outlined the application of the mediation hypothesis to problem solving and learning of meaningful material, have reviewed the mediation hypothesis itself and some of the studies which pertain to it, and have suggested that the study of language will both require and lead to the further illumination of the process. I see the mediation hypothesis as a most powerful approach to the many problems of organization which research and theory encounter as they move into cognitive and other complex research areas. As research and theory develop, I believe that the mediation hypothesis can become a rigorously developed and operationally defined conception, which will have profound and useful implications for the analysis, description, and measurement of stimulus equivalence and of response selection and direction.

REFERENCES

1. Bartlett, F. C. *Remembering: A Study in Experimental and Social Psychology*. New York: Cambridge University Press, 1932.
2. Birge, J. S. "The Role of Verbal Responses in Transfer." Ph.D. dissertation, Yale University, 1941.
3. Bousfield, W. A. The occurrence of clustering in the recall of randomly arranged associates. *J. Gen. Psychol.*, 1953, 49: 229-40.
4. Cofer, C. N. An analysis of errors made in the learning of prose materials. *J. Exp. Psychol.*, 1943, 32: 399-410.
5. Dollard, J., and Miller, N. E. *Personality and Psychotherapy: An Analysis in Terms of Learning, Thinking, and Culture*. New York: McGraw-Hill Book Co., 1950.
6. Hilgard, E. R., and Marquis, D. G. *Conditioning and Learning*. New York: Appleton-Century, 1940.
7. Howes, D., and Osgood, C. E. On the combination of associative probabilities in linguistic contexts. *Amer. J. Psychol.*, 1954, 67: 241-58.
8. Hull, C. L. Knowledge and purpose as habit mechanisms. *Psychol. Rev.*, 1930, 37: 511-25.
9. Jeffrey, W. E. The effects of verbal and nonverbal responses in mediating an instrumental act. *J. Exp. Psychol.*, 1953, 45: 327-33.

10. Jenkins, J. J., and Russell, W. A. Associative clustering during recall. *J. Abnorm. Soc. Psychol.*, 1952, 47: 818-21.

11. Katona, G. *Organizing and Memorizing: Studies in the Psychology of Learning and Teaching*. New York: Columbia University Press, 1940.

12. Maier, N. R. F. Reasoning in humans: II. The solution of a problem and its appearance in consciousness. *J. Comp. Psychol.*, 1931, 12: 181-94.

13. Maslow, A. H. *Motivation and Personality*. New York: Harper & Brothers, 1954.

14. May, M. A. Experimentally acquired drives. *J. Exp. Psychol.*, 1948, 38: 66-77.

15. Miller, G. A. The magic number seven plus or minus two. Invited address, annual meeting, Eastern Psychological Association, 1955.

16. Miller, G. A., and Selfridge, J. A. Verbal context and the recall of meaningful material. *Amer. J. Psychol.*, 1950, 63: 176-85.

17. Osgood, C. E. *Method and Theory in Experimental Psychology*. New York: Oxford University Press, 1953.

18. ———. The nature and measurement of meaning. *Psychol. Bull.*, 1952, 49: 197-237.

19. Postman, L. Learned principles of organization in memory. *Psychol. Monogr.*, 1954, 68: No. 3 (whole No. 374).

20. Razran, G. H. S. A quantitative study of meaning by a conditioned salivary technique (semantic conditioning). *Science*, 1939, 90: 89-90.

21. Riess, B. F. Semantic conditioning involving the galvanic skin reflex. *J. Exp. Psychol.*, 1940, 26: 238-40.

22. Russell, W. A., and Storms, L. H. Implicit verbal chaining in paired-associate learning. *J. Exp. Psychol.*, 1955, 49: 287-93.

23. Schachtel, E. On memory and childhood amnesia. In Mullahy, P. (ed.), *A Study of Interpersonal Relations: New Contributions to Psychiatry*. New York: Hermitage Press, 1949.

24. Shipley, W. C. Indirect conditioning. *J. Gen. Psychol.*, 1935, 12: 337-57.

25. Wickens, D. D., and Briggs, G. E. Mediated stimulus generalization as a factor in sensory pre-conditioning. *J. Exp. Psychol.*, 1951, 42: 197-200.

26. Yarczower, M. "Generalization Along an Association Gradient Mediated by Synonymity." M. A. thesis, University of Maryland, 1955.

INTERACTION BETWEEN METHODS AND MODELS IN SOCIAL PSYCHOLOGY

HAROLD GUETZKOW

The author is specially indebted to two of his colleagues, Drs. James G. March and Herbert A. Simon, with whom he has worked intensively in the development of an inventory of propositions about organizational behavior under a special grant from The Behavioral Sciences Division of the Ford Foundation while this paper was being prepared.

MOST people agree that *how* you go about getting answers to your questions influences the answers you get. In fact, our methods sometimes gain momentum of their own, asking their own questions. Vice versa, the questions you ask also influence the methodology you use in getting answers. Methodological developments seem dependent on the models of social behavior we use in asking our questions. I believe it may be useful to conceive this review of current trends and developments in methodology in social psychology as an interaction between methods and models.

In this discussion I use the term "model" to mean a system of hypotheses being tested by the researcher in his investigations. The system consists of variables which are hypothesized to be interrelated in particular ways. Sometimes within the model we find quasi-isolable subsets of hypotheses—these I call "mechanisms." These systems of hypotheses sometimes are well organized and explicit. At other times you find them implicit and unsystemized—hardly designable as a "model." There is nothing uncommon in using the term "methodology" to mean the techniques and principles of procedure and analysis employed in research investigations.

The analysis consists of three parts. First, I explore the impact of methodology upon theory building. Second, I consider the inverse relationship, the effects of theories upon methods. And third, I discuss the development of models about methodology.

THE IMPACT OF METHODS UPON THEORY BUILDING

Social psychologists have borrowed freely in their methods from other psychologists and from their fellow students of behavior—the sociologists, anthropologists, and political scientists. For some time we also have borrowed from the statisticians, and more recently we have been using the results of the labor of mathematicians. Sometimes we have borrowed quite uncritically; sometimes we have borrowed and then developed the methodologies with considerable imagination. Let me mention examples of this diffusion of methodology into social psychology, with the objective of coming to a generalization about the impact this process of borrowing and extrapolation has had upon the construction of hypotheses in social psychology.

Borrowing from Other Psychologists. Social psychologists have gained depth in their research by borrowing projective techniques from the clinical psychologists. The application of these techniques extends from such time-honored areas of study in social psychology as attitudes to the new frontier or group processes. Social psychological researches involving projective techniques have yielded a number of new variables. For example, Horwitz and Cartwright[14] have developed a sketch to which the group as a whole gives a projective response. Their application yielded new variables which may be used in describing group operations, such as "group nondefensiveness" and "group distractability." In any developing discipline, the isolation and measurement of significant variables is the foundation to adequate theory building. Perhaps most important, the new variables seem to come from the new data obtained through the projective techniques, not from rigidly preconceived notions about the nature of social psychological processes.

Social psychologists have gained sharpness in their variables by borrowing techniques from the psychometricians. In the area of attitudes, the use of factor analysis has yielded reduction of a myriad of particular measurements to a more basic structure, as exemplified in Eysenck's[8] factorization of R (radicalism-conservatism and T (tender-minded–tough-minded). This borrowing of factor analysis has also been extended to other areas, as the work by Cattell, Stice, and Saunders[6] in factoring some ninety-three measures made on eighty groups, each consisting of ten persons. Here again, one notes the tendency for the borrowed techniques to yield new variables. In the Illinois group's work, to continue with the same example, at least two new factors characterizing the group (rather than the individual) were produced: a "group elation" factor representing situationally engendered excitement, and "intelligent role interaction," the propensity of groups to handle intellectual group problems with adaptability in both "group aspiration" level and "adjustment of individual interests to those reached in group discussion."

Borrowing from Other Social Sciences. But social psychologists have borrowed not only from their fellow psychologists. We have borrowed from workers in other fields. For example, our increasing use and development of techniques of content analysis have been taken from the political scientist and journalist.[21] To avoid the narrowness of connotation which surrounds their origin in the analysis of the contents of newspapers and political speeches as mass media, the term "coding procedures" will be applied to the methodology of content analysis.[1] The fundamental task in coding is to transform a set of unitized symbolic responses—be they oral, written, or gestural—into classifications which may be counted and then quantitatively analyzed. Techniques for transforming raw data which seem highly qualitative into quantitative data which may be manipulated statistically gives tremendous leverage in working with social phenomena. One of the important features of coding systems is that they often are developed a posteriori. The experimenters examine their data and then inductively attempt to establish classifications. Heyns[12] and Carter[5] have both developed multivariable descriptions of problem solving in this way. In some fourteen codes about group process I have examined, I counted altogether

387 variables which had been established through content analysis techniques. The strength of coding methodologies rests in their ability to encompass something of the richness of social behavior. Again, in this borrowing and extrapolation of technique, its central effect has been to aid in the isolation of variables.

The Development of Sociometry. We social psychologists tend not to be developing a methodology of our own. Perhaps closest to an indigenous development is our collaboration with the sociologists in utilizing sociometry. We social psychologists have done so much with sociometry because our central interest is in the nature of interpersonal relations. Although its invention in the 1930's by J. L. Moreno was embedded in theoretical considerations, sociometry has grown as a technique, almost without roots in theory. Its development is an example of my earlier assertion that sometimes our methods gain momentum of their own. Sociometry is a descriptive device. As Lindzey and Borgatta put it, it is "a means of assessing the attractions, or attractions and repulsions, within a given group."[28, p. 407] It is used in a variety of ways by different system builders, quite apart from the theoretical context in which it had its origin.

There has been a prodigious proliferation of ways of ascertaining the sociometry of groups. This variation has taken two primary forms—ways of ascertaining the social perceptions of the members of the group about each other, and attempts at objective estimates of the social structure of the group by observing the volume of interactions which occur between group members.

Although the variations in asking about social perceptions have been ingenious, they fundamentally are all special cases of attitudinal measurement. At times the variation is primitive, asking for "choice" responses —yes or no—rather than ratings on a continuum of attraction-repulsion. With our addiction as social psychologists to attitudinal measurement, it is little wonder we lost no time in endorsing this form of sociometry. It is a most inexpensive way of studying groups. The incommensurate nature of the frames of reference used by different members of a group in making their choices seems not to disturb too many of my colleagues. Some even argue that the respondent should use those particular beliefs and irrational criteria which he has been spending his whole lifetime in developing, as it is just those criteria he does use in making his choices in real social groups. Perhaps this conviction indicates why so little work has been done to ascertain the underlying components from which sociometric judgments are built.

Contrasting to sociometry conceived as social perception is the endeavor to measure the attractions and repulsions of the members of the group through their actual contacts with each other. Observational tallying of contacts yield objective data. Quasi-objective results may be obtained by asking each member of the group for estimates of the kind and extent of contact he has with the others. This tool has been used in the researches of the Institute for Social Research by Weiss and Jacobson[38] with considerable success in describing the structure of administrative groups.

But whether the sociometric data are based on observations or respondent perceptions, there is difficulty in making interpretations of the data, once they have been gathered. Much interpretation of the sociometric choices is done by drawing geometric diagrams of the so-called "group structure." Because a given set of "choices" may be drawn in a number of alternative ways, there is disagreement among the diagramers. These disagreements have prompted use of preferred ordering procedures, which are possible when the data are tabulated in matrix form. By performing quite simple mathematical operations on the matrices, one can identify subgroups and cliques. Once the rules for manipulation have been established, there is little disagreement among interpreters.

These methodological developments toward reduction in ambiguity of interpretation have been paralleled by the invention of indexes—from simple ratios to complicated formulae—by which the voluminous sociometric data may be expressed more simply.[31] These indexes are usually developed on an a priori basis and are asserted to measure such individaul and/or group characteristics as cohesiveness, emotional expansiveness, and social status. This tendency to develop more variables—in one report I was able to count twelve such indexes—is a strong trend—similar to our tendency to delineate variables when we borrow our methodology from other psychologists and other social behaviorists.

As soon as one begins interpreting the sociometric data, one meets the problem as to whether or not these various indexes of attraction and repulsion are not mere random variations. Out of such questions came one of the few theoretical endeavors in sociometry to do more than enumerate more variables. Leeman[23] was able to construct a model which predicts sociometric relations among people. He hypothesized that at first persons in small, face-to-face groups do meet on a random basis. But as a result of their initial contacts, they begin taking on likes and dislikes. These likes and dislikes lead to further interaction, which in turn accentuates or changes the earlier attractions and repulsions. By using this kind of probabilistic model, Leeman was able to work through predictions for four-man groups. When he tried to develop sociometric structures for larger groups, the mathematics became too difficult to handle. Yet even his theory originated from classical assumptions about stochastic processes and in a sense derives from the statistical methodology.

Note the nature of these methodological developments in sociometry. The methodology originated at the border of clinical psychology and sociology. Its growth has been away from theoretical roots, tending to exhibit an almost unrestrained production of variables. The plethora of data induced a search for their simplication by the construction of indexes. Attempts to differentiate the group choice from random choices resulted in stochastic model building. An overview of sociometry leaves one with the impression that scientific history is repeating itself—the imperative application of the attitude methodology in the 1920's and 1930's to almost all topics in social psychology is being re-enacted in the 1940's and 1950's in the extensive use of sociometric methodology to a wide area of problems.

As I noted earlier, methodologies seem to gain a momentum of their own—sociometry has it.

Proposition about the Impact of Methods upon Theory Building. This brief survey of methodological trends in social psychology indicates there is little indigenous methodology. We have borrowed profusely from our colleagues in clinical and experimental psychology and from the statisticians and psychometricians. We have borrowed from outside our discipline, from the anthropologists, sociologists, and political behaviorists. And in this borrowing, we have exhibited an all-pervasive trend, which may be asserted as a proposition: *In social psychology the borrowing and extrapolation of methodologies are more conducive to the delineation of variables than to the organization of variables into systems.* When we lean on others for our methodologies and let these methodologies guide our researches, the methodologies tend to drive us toward the construction and proliferation of variables rather than toward their assembly into models.

THE IMPACT OF MODELS UPON THE DEVELOPMENT OF METHODOLOGY

Models influence methods, just as methods influence theory construction. Thus, my central thesis: there is interaction between models and methods. In surveying the influence our models have upon our methods in social psychology, I want to separate the influence the substance or content of our theories has upon our methodologies from the influence the form of our theories has upon our methods.

The Influence of the Content of our Theories. The social psychologist's concern with the theory of social perception has developed his methodology for working with multiperson relations. Recent interest in such concepts as social sensitivity and empathy has developed methodologies in which the simple procedure of measuring A's attitude toward object X no longer suffices. Instead, our procedures become multilevel. We become as interested in B's perception of A as in A's perception of B. And then our methodology is pushed further when we inquire of A's perception of B's perception of A. An example of the extension of the traditional methods is found in Tagiuri, Blake, and Bruner's[36] work on determinants of perception of feeling in others. Using a more complicated methodology, these investigators were able to discover that an individual identifies those who like him more accurately than those who dislike him or feel neutral toward him. Because of their interest in the social perceptions involved in interpersonal relations, their methods involved sets of perceptions at different levels.[35]

Another area in which our substantive interests have forced methodological growth is in the use of personality characteristics to predict group interactions. Because so many personality variables describe quasi-stable ways in which an individual relates to others, our methodologies in social psychology are coming to include measures of personal characteristics. There are many examples of this methodological trend. Perhaps Schutz's recent success[33] in creating high and low productivity in groups on the basis of member compatibility is the most vivid. Oriented in terms of Bion's theory, Schutz assessed such personality characteristics as the extent of the dependency each person feels toward the leader of the group, and the extent to which each enjoys personal interrelations with others. After he had measured these characteristics in each person, he constructed experimental groups of compatible and incompatible persons. Compatible groups, for example, might be composed of many persons who depended on structured leadership and but one person who wanted such leadership. Incompatible groups might be constructed by placing two persons who wanted structured leadership along with others who didn't want any leadership but were much more interested in easy personal relations with others. Substantive interest in the effects of personal characteristics upon group functioning has developed recently a methodology for the composition of groups on the basis of personality characteristics.

As we social psychologists center our attention upon interaction in groups, we need methodologies which enable us to observe these interactions. In one sense the observational techniques themselves are not new, as the child psychologists have long used them to record the activity of the individual child in social situations. But the social psychologists' theoretical emphasis on interaction has demanded the development of observational methodologies which encompass the activity of the whole group of individuals, not just a single member. Because we are no longer centrally interested in attitudes, they are now measured in the course of group interaction, either directly by interpolated questionnaires, or indirectly from spontaneous verbal expressions. Attitude assessment is still necessary when attitudes are used as intervening variables in the prediction of interaction. Students of Kurt Lewin have been most ingenious in developing methodologies of observation which will allow their theories to be tested. For example, they have learned how to slow down the process of interaction by using written messages instead of oral messages. The combination of assessment of intervening variables, techniques for slowing down the rate of interaction, and simultaneous observation of all persons in interaction—this combination of methodologies has resulted from the new content of social psychology.

Along with other students of human behavior, the social psychologist is concerned about the extent to which his theories are culture-bound. To check whether his theories are dependent upon the particular culture in which he happens to be researching, the social psychologist more recently has made efforts to extend his studies across cultures. This theoretical concern demands development of our methodology. Buchanan and Cantril[4] recently faced the intricate problem of multilanguage questionnaires in their cross-national study of tensions for UNESCO. In carrying out experiments across cultures, we have much to learn to make the meaning of the experimental situation for subjects in one country comparable in its meaning for those in another country, as a recent experimental expedition indicates.[16]

As our theoretical interests broaden, our methodologies tend to develop, too. But the substance of our systems of hypotheses is not the only route by which our theory influences our methodology. The procedures we use are also powerfully influenced by the very form of the theory we use in our social psychological research endeavors.

The Influence of the Form of the Models. There has been an important trend within recent years toward more complicated models. Traditionally, the social psychologist has worked with a two-variable model, in which one variable is considered predictor of the second variable, a criterion. This model is illustrated in Figure 1*a*. Such two-variable models have limitations, not the least of which is the small proportion of total variance usually accounted for by the single predictor. This has encouraged the use of multiple predictors, so that a more respectable proportion of the variance in the criterion might be predicting variables. A diagram of this development of the basic model is given in Figure 1*b*.

As theory builders face their empirical data, they need refinements in the forms of their models. For example, in working with the "multiple-predictors—single-criterion" model (Figure 1*b*), it becomes apparent that two or more predictors might exercise their effects upon the outcome, either separately or in conjunction with each other. This means the social psychologist must use methodologies which disentangle the interaction effects among his predictors. Bray's experiments[3] on conformity in the autokinetic situation illustrate the extensions in methodology which the form of the theory demands. In his experiments

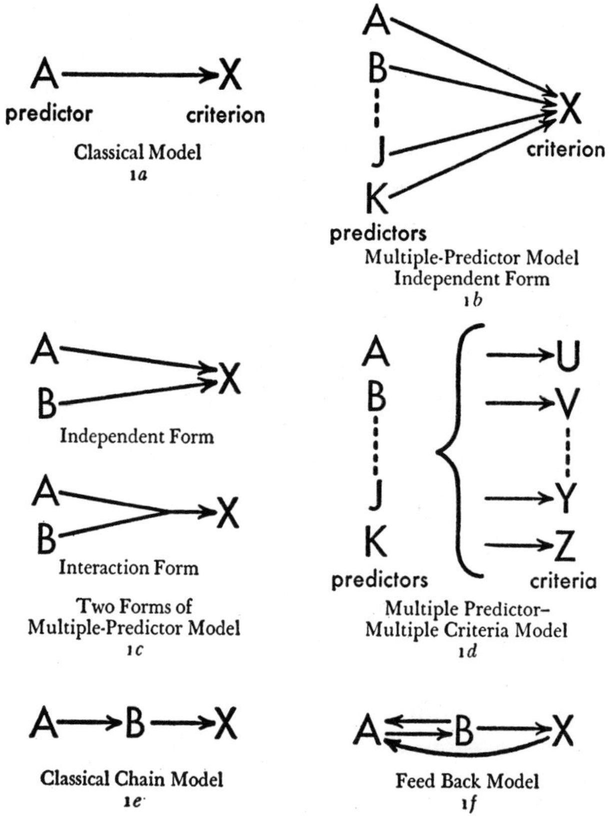

FIGURE 1. Trends in the Development of the Form of Models

two persons are asked to judge the apparent movement of a stationary pin point of light. One of each pair of judges is of a different racial or ethnic group from that of the other. When Bray used a simple predictor-criterion model (Figure 1*a*), he failed to predict the amount of conformity in his experimental situation from the pre-experimental measure of prejudice. However, when he introduced another variable—a personality measure—he was able to raise the prediction to the significance level. Because of the interaction effects between this personal characteristic (nervousness, as measured by Guilford's GAMIN scale) and the attitude (racial prejudice), measured before the subject was placed in the experimental situation, the criterion could be predicted only by considering the conjunctive nature of the relationship between the two predictors. Thus, it is necessary to specify two forms of the multiple-predictor model, as indicated in Figure 1*c*.

There also has been a recent trend toward the use of multiple criteria, rather than a single criterion. When social psychologists focused on the attitude, its prediction as a solitary variable was meaningful. As social psychologists become more and more interested in the functioning of groups, it has become difficult to stay interested in but one facet of the outcome of the group's behavior. Instead, he becomes interested in a number of simultaneously achieved consequences of the interrelations among persons. The basic form of the model is exhibited in Figure 1*d*. An example of this trend is found in the Conference Research field study on decision-making groups reported by Marquis, Heyns, and myself.[29] During the early part of our work on this project, an attempt was made to settle upon a single criterion, one which might encompass the major results of the decision-making conferences. In the end we made predictions about three outcomes—group productivity, member satisfaction, and final disagreement among members in a decision-making conference. In this work, we used a large number of variables as predictors. It was found that some of these predictors were uniquely related to but one of the outcomes; other predictors related to two or three of the outcomes. This more complicated form of our theory had its impact, of course, upon our methodology. One of its most inconvenient consequences, methodologically, is its demand that a large number of variables be measured all at the same time. In the Conference Research project, this meant simultaneous observation of each decision-making conference by three highly trained observers and a willingness on the part of hundreds of subjects to submit themselves to an array of questionnaires before the conference began and both immediately and some weeks after their conference had been concluded.

Another increase in complexity of the form of the model occurs when the social psychologist transfers his interest from the person in a social situation to the interactions of the social situation. As the social psychologist attempts to represent more of the total social situation, he in intrigued with the chain of variables which seems to be involved, that A causes B which in turn produces X (Figure 1*e*). Because all three variables exist simultaneously, it now becomes important to make careful checks on the time relations among the changes in the three variables. And as the importance of circular casual processes is recognized, attention is given to the study of feed-back effects. The introduction of "loops" into a simple chain model, as illustrated in Figure 1*f*, further complicates the methodology needed to check the hypotheses. Instead of being able

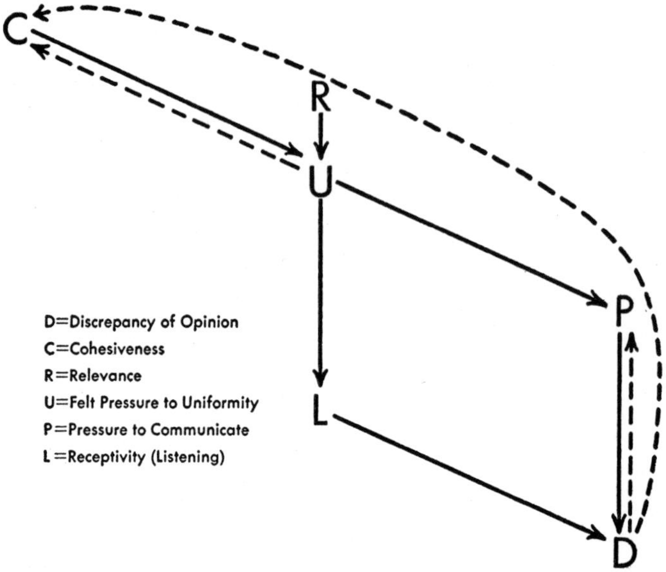

FIGURE 2. Festinger Model

to merely observe the system in a "steady state," the experimenter now must adopt a methodology which observes the system in "change," so that the effects of the feed-back mechanisms within the system may be studied.

These last two trends toward concern about chains and feedbacks are vividly illustrated in the experiments of Festinger and his associates.[9] Figure 2 presents a simplified model[34] of part of Festinger's theory of conformity. The solid lines in this figure represent the direct chain relationships among the variables; the dotted lines represent the feed-back loops which are hypothesized in his models. The elaborate experimental techniques which Festinger and his associates have so ingeniously devised to test these hypotheses stem from the complicated form of their theory.

These trends in the forms of the model seem to have at least four important effects upon the methodological development within social psychology. They are:

1. Increased complexity of the form of the model occurs when the social psychologist transfers his interest from the person within a social situation to the interactions of the social situation itself. When social psychology is the psychology of the *individual* in social situations about social objects, the intervening variables involved in the theory are usually hypothetical constructs inside the person, to which access often is denied to the experimenter unless he becomes neurophysiologist. But when the object of the research is the *group* itself, it becomes possible to make interpolated measures of these intervening processes. An example of such methodological advance is found in Schacter's experimental work[32] on communication in groups, in which he measured the pressure to communicate (see Figure 2) by counting the messages which were sent at particular times in the course of the group's development. Important use of measurement of the intervening variable is found in Thibault's work[37] on the cohesiveness of underprivileged groups. Through the use of presession sociometrics, he was able to identify central *vs.* peripheral members in his experimental group. The effects of the experimental treatment were differential, depending upon the intervening centrality-peripherality of the subject. By having measured this intervening variable, Thibault was able to trace its effects empirically.

2. If the interaction effects among variables are great, it is imperative to use more laboratory, contrived situations in order to isolate and unmask the effects of particular mechanisms. These subsystems often are embedded into a total system, so that their effects are often disguised. Although there has been a long-term trend toward the use of the laboratory for analyzing the small, face-to-face group, in the past five years this trend has been accentuated. The laboratory experiment now includes the larger group, in which the interpersonal relations are indirect, rather than face to face. In my Organizational Behavior Laboratory in the Graduate School of Industrial Administration, we[11] have been able to develop a "quasi-company" in which to explore relationships between groups, as well as the indirect relationships among individuals within groups. In our two-department company—consisting of a production group and a sales group—we have a methodology which allows us to watch the longitudinal development of the company toward equilibrium. The procedure involves interrelations among six persons over a period of twelve hours, the operation itself being interrupted by simulated "shifts" and "week ends." Perhaps the most spectacular development in this direction comes out of RAND's Systems Research Laboratory. Kennedy and his colleagues[19] have there contrived an information processing organization consisting of thirty-six persons, which has an experimental group life of 185 hours!

3. Our new theoretical models are forcing methodologies which allow us to capture the nature of systems-in-change, rather than systems-at-rest. To watch sys-

tems change over time, we are giving more emphasis to longitudinal studies, both in the field and in the laboratory. From this need has come the panel-interview technique. Lazarsfeld and his associates[18] have long recognized the importance of questioning respondents periodically over considerable intervals of time to nail down the locus of change in voting behavior.[2] Little is known about the effects of repetition of an interview upon the respondent's actual behavior. The essence of the methodological change is a shift from a technique which involves thin time-slices to one involving very thick time-slices. When our focus was on processes which occurred with very short time-lags, as is the case in attitude work, near-simultaneous measures of predictor and criterion were justifiable. Now, as we focus on group behaviors involving considerable delays and feed-back processes, it is imperative to study the systems involved over longer periods of time.

4. To this point the noted impact of the forms of the models has been largely upon the experimental and field designs employed and the observational procedures used. But there has been an important methodological impact of the forms upon the language in which the models are conceived—in the use of mathematics. When one works with dynamic rather than static systems—that is, when one works with chains of variables and feedback among the variables in multi-predictor-multicriteria systems—the conceptualization of the model often becomes quite difficult and demands special language tools for model building. The use of mathematics for conceptualization is quite different from the use of psychometric and statistical

tools in the delineation of variables, as was mentioned earlier. Mathematicians have developed ways of handling systems containing both simultaneous and delayed relations among variables. For example, the Festinger model diagrammed in Figure 2 may be written as a set of equations:[34]

$$\frac{dD}{dt} = f\,[P(t), L(t), D(t)], \qquad [1.1]$$

$$P(t) = P\,[D(t), U(t)], \qquad [1.2]$$

$$L(t) = L[U(t)], \qquad [1.3]$$

$$\frac{dC}{dt} = g\,[D(t), U(t), C(t)], \qquad [1.4]$$

$$U(t) = U[C(t), R]. \qquad [1.5]$$

The definitions of the variables are given in the legend of Figure 2. As Simon and I have demonstrated, even though the equations are of a very abstract and general form, certain consequences from them can be derived. In addition, they have been helpful in clarifying what relations have been tested by the experiments to date—and which ones still need testing. When one works through these relationships in the language of mathematics, one appreciates how little the vernacular aids in reducing theoretical confusion.

Proposition about the Impact of Theory Building upon Methods. Thus, there are two very important ways in which the nature of the model influences the methodology of the social psychologists. The content of the model itself—the kind of phenomena which occupies the center of the researcher's attention—has its impact upon the methods used. In addition, the

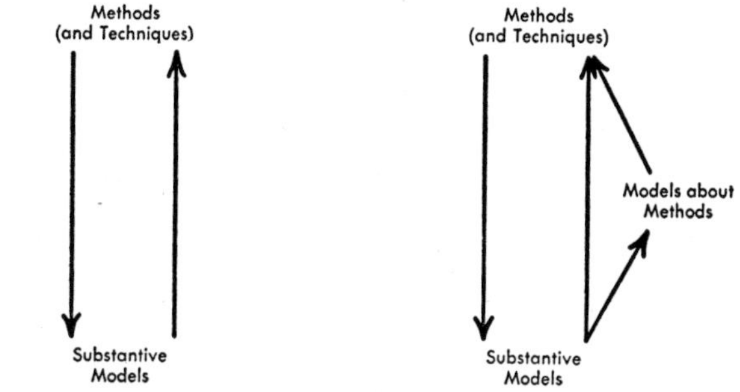

Interaction of
Methods and
Substantive Models
3a

Interaction of
Methods with both Substantive
and Methodological Models
3b

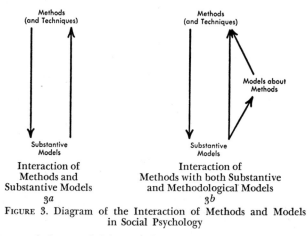

FIGURE 3. Diagram of the Interaction of Methods and Models in Social Psychology

form of the model has an important impact upon the methodologies employed in the investigations. Perhaps this current trend may be asserted in the following proposition: *In social psychology the development of models creates more extensions of methodology than methodological developments themselves promote extension of the theoretical models.*

As the reader probably already has noted, the two propositions I have asserted to this point constitute a model in themselves. It has been diagrammed in Figure *3a*.

TRENDS TOWARD A SCIENCE OF METHODOLOGY

My omission of two important fields of methodological advance—psychometrics and statistics—has been intentional. Trends in these fields are having a profound influence upon our methods in social psychology. In psychometrics, for instance, there is intensive exploration of ways to relax the cardinality assumptions in working with measurement scales. In statistics, the rapid development of nonparametric techniques is important to social psychologists whose data simply do not exhibit the basic characteristics demanded by our ordinary statistical devices. But because the effects of these methodological advances are not peculiar to social psychology, they seem not within the scope of my assignment.

But the advances in psychometrics and statistics suggest that the current trends in the methodology of social psychology include an energetic attempt to codify our methods—and even to do research on our research methods and our application procedures. Discussion of these trends is essential to completion of the survey and follows herewith.

Codification of the Methodology. As a discipline becomes more mature, it tends to systematize its methods and to standardize its vocabulary. Attempts to present the total methodology now in use by social psychologists constitute a new trend. In 1951, Jahoda, Deutsch, and Cook published their *Research Methods in Social Relations.*[17] Although this work tended to concentrate on methods useful in the analysis of prejudice, it has been widely used by scholars as a methodological handbook for work in other areas of social psychology. In 1953 social behavorists at the University of Michigan wrote essays covering the gamut in their *Research Methods of the Behavioral Sciences.*[10] In 1954 Lindzey's *Handbook of Social Psychology*[27] included some nine chapters on research methods, ranging all the way from experimental design to observational techniques.

Last year, a specialized monograph appeared on *The Miniature Social Situation,*[39] examining one of social psychology's most unique methods, the experimenter-contrived interaction system. And in 1955 Lazarsfeld and Rosenberg released *The Language of Social Research.*[22] None of these books is a rigorous codification of our methods; their appearance indicates, however, a trend toward maturation of our methodology.

Models about Research Methods. An outstanding example of the trend toward better theories about our methodology is found in Hyman's *Interviewing in Social Research.*[15] These theories are backed by empirical work, just as we support our theories about the substance of social psychology by studies in the field and laboratory. To understand one's interviewing methodology, one must have a theory about the relationship of the interviewer to the respondent, about the way in which the respondent himself affects the interviewer, and an analysis of the effects of the situational variables which provide the context for the interview. Hyman and his associates have dug into these matters. For example, they have explored the systematic effects of group membership disparities between the interviewer and respondent. They have conducted experimental studies in the laboratory and then checked the transferability of their theory into field situations on such important methodological matters as the impact of interviewee anonymity and survey sponsorship. They have researched even the degree of structuredness of the interview situation. It seems to me they have made a most important step forward in building a model about our research methods—and then done research on the model itself to check its congruence with fact. As our models of our methodologies improve, we gain more control over our errors. A theory about our methods gives toeholds from which we may invent better methodologies.

The interview is not the only technique about which we are concerned. An important trend toward theory about methods is noticeable in the area of our observational procedures. Heyns, Lippitt, and Zander have pressed forward to conceptualization of fundamental dimensions in terms of which different observational systems can be compared.[13, 40] For example, one important difference between systems is found in the size of the unit used in the observation of social behavior. They also describe differences in the level of inference which is demanded of the observers, ranging from high levels involving much interpretation of behavior to low levels in which simple, more objective acts are recorded by the observers. This attempt to establish dimensions for comparison of observational systems is a necessary prerequisite for research on the empirical consequences of different characteristics of the system. Although to date there has been little empirical research done on the nature of observational systems, this attempt to construct such theory presages further methodological model building and testing.

There is a nascent trend toward more theory about the effects of the observer upon the experimental situation. As social psychologists we have long been aware of the "Western Electric" effect—as so vividly dramatized in the Hawthorne studies in the 1930's. We are now challenging the dictum that "the subject soon becomes accustomed to the presence of the observers, so that their influence is inconsequential after a few minutes of observation." Polansky, Lippitt, and Redl[30] demonstrated in their studies of contagious behavior that after a few weeks of continuous observation, the observers themselves become an important part of the interaction process itself. In this case, instead of becoming less and less noticed, the observers at the end of three weeks became targets of hostility which was generated by the ambiguity of the observers' role in the total situation. Some experimenters now include questions about the observers and the subjects' perceptions of the purpose of the experiment in their research inquiries. This trend toward systematic study of the effects of our methods upon our researches is not strong—but it is important and will probably gain momentum.

Models about Application Methods. As social psychology matures, its contributions to our educational, industrial, and civic life become greater and greater. Our important contribution to the Supreme Court's desegregation decision in 1954—via our documentation of the psychological effects of separate school systems—aids us in becoming aware of the application potential of our research findings.[7] But to date, there has been little systematic thinking about the methods we are using in making our applications. In 1946, David Krech[20] edited an issue of *The Journal of Social Issues* on "Action and Research—A Challenge." In 1949, Alexander Leighton,[24] psychiatrist and anthropologist, described the use of social behavior theory in our relations with the Japanese—on the home front with our internees and on the military-political front with our enemies. In 1951, Lerner and Lasswell[25] gathered a set of papers on *The Policy Sciences* which included a few essays on the problems involved in applying natural and social sciences to problems of administrative policy in national affairs. But we social psychologists have not given this problem the serious thought it deserves.

To this point in my discussion I have surveyed current trends; in ending my presentation may I have leave to argue that we should accelerate a trend? It is my contention that we need a model about the application process itself. Such a model will need to handle two basic problems—variable identification and estimation of parameters.

At first glance, it would seem that the problem of variable identification would be the easiest. But perhaps it is not. In social psychology we are plagued by the fact that two or three seemingly alternative ways of measuring a given variable result in measures which have little correlation among themselves, as Libo[26] so dramatically illustrated in his attempt to operationalize the meaning of group cohesiveness. It often is difficult to reidentify a variable from our theory when it is embodied in the messy reality of the natural world.

But suppose our methodology is adequately developed to handle this variable identification problem. Then, we have another—that is, estimating the strength of the variables in a given multivariate situation. This may be easier to do than making the original identification. If two or more factors influence the outcome in a given application, it is important to estimate with some accuracy the parameters which tell the differential weights to be assigned to the variables in producing their effects. Although the basic models may hold from one application to another, there may be dramatic shifts in the importance of the components. If the same parametic weights are applied across the board, the application often will be abortive.

Perhaps an analogy from physical engineering will be helpful in allowing us to understand the methodological problem we social psychologists face when we act as social engineers. The civil engineer who applies the equations which constitute the model for bridge building must decide in each case how much traffic his bridge will need to bear; he must make detailed studies of the nature of the foundation upon which his structure will be resting; he must understand the meteorological stresses to which his bridge will be subjected. Although the fundamental models of bridge building have been well formulated and tested, his extensive studies of the particular parameters which apply in this particular application is essential to successful use of bridge-building theory. Likewise in social psychology, as our substantive models are developed with more and more adequacy, we will need to develop better methods for making application of the models in particular situations.

Proposition on the Impact of Models about Methodology upon the Methods and Models of Social Psychology. It is reasonable to ask whether the models about our methodology in social psychology actually differ from the substantive models we develop as the content of our research. It would seem to me that there is no important difference between the two sets of models. Because our behavior as researchers is merely a special subset of the totality of human behavior, our substantive models must include as special cases our models about methodology. This relationship has already been exhibited in this discourse, as for example, in Hyman's use of reference group theory (a part of the substantive theory of social psychology) in developing his methodological theory (about the relation of respondent to interviewer) about the interview.

But the distinction, even if not fundamental, seems strategically important in the present state of our discipline, as is asserted in the following proposition: *Better substantive models of social (and other) psychological processes aid in the development of better theories about methodologies, which in turn, help to produce better methods leading to better models of social psychological processes.* The proposition is diagrammed in Figure 3*b*. We social psychologists will make faster progress if we accelerate the application of our basic, substantive models to the development of more adequate theories about our methodology and techniques.

SUMMARY

May I briefly summarize my review of current trends in the methodology of social psychology. There has been much borrowing of methods from others—from the other fields of psychology and from the domains of other behavioral scientists. There has been much modification of these borrowed methods, with considerable extrapolation of their use into quite new situations. But only in our development of sociometry has social psychology a methodology which seems to have a momentum of its own—but this methodology has been borrowed, too. Our borrowed techniques and procedures have resulted largely in the proliferation of new variables, not in the establishment of new theories.

Inversely, our development of theory in social psychology has resulted in the elaboration of the methods we use. This effect has its roots in both the substance or content of our theory and in the form of our models which comprise the theory. Thus, there is an interaction between methods and models in social psychology—the methods yield variables which can be introduced into our models; these models in turn demand the elaboration of more intricate methodologies.

Given this interaction between methods and models, how might the speed of development of our methodologies be accelerated? It is proposed that the development of more adequate substantive models about the methodologies would be most strategic. Our methods cannot be stronger than our insight into our models, because the methods are special applications of a more general theory of social psychology. The recent trend toward the codification of our methods procedures should be encouraged. Our effort to understand our research procedures should be complemented by effort to build a model about our application methods.

REFERENCES

1. Berelson, B. *Content Analysis in Communication Research.* Glencoe, Illinois: The Free Press, 1952.
2. Berelson, B., Lazarsfeld, P. F., and McPhee, W. N. *A Study of Opinion Formation in a Presidential Campaign.* Chicago: University of Chicago Press, 1954.
3. Bray, D. W. The prediction of behavior from two attitude scales. *J. Abnorm. Soc. Psychol.,* 1950, 45: 64-84.
4. Buchanan, W., and Cantril, H. *How Nations See Each Other.* Urbana: University of Illinois Press, 1953.
5. Carter, L., Haythorn, W., Meirowitz, B., and Lanzetta, J. The relation of categorizations and ratings in the observation of group behavior. *Hum. Rel.,* 1951, 4: 239-54.
6. Cattell, R. B., Saunders, D. R., and Stice, G. F. The dimensions of syntality in small groups: I. The neonate group. *Hum. Rel.,* 1953, 6: 331-56.
7. Clark, K. B. Desegregation: An appraisal of the evidence. *Journal of Social Issues,* 1953, IX, No. 4, 1-68.
8. Eysenck, H. J. *The Structure of Human Personality.* London: Methuen, 1953.
9. Festinger, L. Informal social communication. *Psychol. Rev.,* 1950, 57: 271-82.
10. Festinger, L., and Katz, D. *Research Methods in the Behavioral Sciences.* New York: Dryden Press, 1953.
11. Guetzkow, H., and Bowes, A. E. *Preliminary Report on the Development of Organizations with a Division of Labor.* Pittsburgh: Carnegie Institute of Technology, 1954.
12. Heyns, R. W. Conference Research Problem-solving Category System. Pp. 378-80 in reference 27.
13. Heyns, R. W., and Lippitt, R. Systematic Observational Techniques. Pp. 370-404 in reference 27.
14. Horwitz, M., and Cartwright, D. A projective method for the diagnosis of group properties. *Hum. Rel.,* 1953, 6: 397-410.
15. Hyman, H. H., *et al. Interviewing in Social Research.* Chicago: University of Chicago Press, 1954.
16. Jacobson, E., and Schachter, S. (eds.). Cross-national research, a case study. *Journal of Social Issues,* 1954, X, No. 4, 68.

17. Jahoda, M., Deutsch, and Cook, W. S. *Research Methods in Social Relations, with Special Reference to Prejudice.* Part One: Basic Processes; Part Two: Selected Techniques. New York: Dryden Press.

18. Kendall, P. L., and Lazarsfeld, P. F. Problem of Survey Analysis. In Merton, R. K., and Lazarsfeld, P. F. (eds.). *Continuities in Social Research.* Glencoe, Illinois: The Free Press, 1950.

19. Kennedy, J. L. *The Systems Research Laboratory and its Program: Description of Experiments.* Biel, Wm. C. I. The Physical and Cultural Environment; Newell, A. II. The Task Environment; Chapman, R. L. III. Data Collection and Processing. *Systems Behavior:* Alexander, L. T. I. The Learning Process; Weiner, M. G. II. The Developmental Process. The Rand Corporation, July 29, 1955.

20. Krech, D. (ed.). Action and research—A challenge. *Journal of Social Issues,* November, 1946, II, No. 4, 79.

21. Lasswell, H. D. *The Language of Politics: Studies in Quantitative Semantics.* New York: Stewart, 1949.

22. Lazarsfeld, P. F., and Rosenberg, M. *The Language of Social Research: A Reader in the Methodology of Social Research.* Glencoe, Illinois: The Free Press, 1955.

23. Leeman, C. P. Patterns of sociometrichoice in small groups: a mathematical model and related experimentation. *Sociometry,* 1952, 15: 220-43.

24. Leighton, A. H. *Human Relations in a Changing World: Observations on the Use of the Social Sciences.* New York: E. P. Dutton, 1949.

25. Lerner, D., and Lasswell, H. D. (eds.). *The Policy Sciences.* Stanford, California: The Stanford University Press, 1951.

26. Libo, L. M. *Measuring Group Cohesiveness.* Ann Arbor, Michigan; Institute for Social Research, University of Michigan, 1953.

27. Lindzey, G. (ed.). *Handbook of Social Psychology.* Boston: Addison-Wesley, 1954. Vol. I, Chapters 7 through 15.

28. Lindzey, G., and Borgatta, E. F. Sociometric Measurement. Pp. 405-48 in reference 27.

29. Marquis, D. G., Guetzkow, H., and Heyns, R. W. A Social Psychological Study of the Decision-making Conference. In Guetzkow, H. (ed.). *Groups, Leadership and Men.* Pittsburgh: Carnegie Press, 1951.

30. Polansky, N., Lippitt, and Redl, F. Problems of interpersonal relations in research on groups. *Hum. Rel.,* 1949, 2: 281-92.

31. Proctor, C. H., and Loomis, C. P. Analysis of Sociometric Data. Pp. 575-81 in reference 17.

32. Schacter, S. Deviation, rejection, and communication. *J. Abnorm. Soc. Psychol.,* 1951, 46: 140-207.

33. Schutz, W. C. *Personal Communication.*

34. Simon, H. A., and Guetzkow, H. A model of short- and long-run mechanisms involved in pressures toward uniformity in groups. *Psychol. Rev.,* 1955, 62: 56-68.

35. Tagiuri, R. Relational analysis; an extension of sociometric method with emphasis upon social perception. *Sociometry,* 1952, 15: 91-104.

36. Tagiuri, R., Blake, R. R., and Bruner, J. S. Some determinants of the perception of positive and negative feelings in others. *J. Abnorm. Soc. Psychol.,* 1953, 48: 585-92.

37. Thibault, J. J. An experimental study of the cohesiveness of underprivileged groups. *Hum. Rel.,* 1950, 3: 251-78.

38. Weiss, R. S., and Jacobson, E. A method for the analysis of the structure of complex organizations. *Amer. Soc. Rev.,* 1955, 20: 661-68.

39. Vinacke, W. E. *The Miniature Social Situation.* Honolulu: University of Hawaii, 1954.

40. Zander, A. Systematic Observation of Small Face-to-Face Groups. Pp. 515-38 in reference 17.

PROCESS AND CONTENT IN PSYCHOLINGUISTICS

JOHN B. CARROLL

INTRODUCTION

NO apologies need be offered for the term psycholinguistics; it is not a newcomer, and it explains itself. Elsewhere[6] I have described psycholinguistics as specifically concerned with the study of the manner in which messages are encoded into a language system by speakers and decoded from that language system by hearers, and a recent monograph edited by Osgood and Sebeok[17] has presented what seems to be a reasonably comprehensive survey of current theories and research problems in psycholinguistics. The availability of this and other excellent surveys leaves me free to focus attention on a few broad methodological considerations and to report several illustrative research investigations.

If psycholinguistics has to do with the encoding and decoding of messages, it must look to the nature and characteristics of the codes which we call languages. It must not neglect the differences between the many language codes in use throughout the world, but, above all, the American psychologist interested in language must become familiar with the linguistic description of the code he uses most of all—the English language. There has been much interest, of late, in what has been called the linguistic relativity hypothesis[10]—the hypothesis espoused by Sapir and particularly by Whorf,[5] that the structure of a particular language in some way constrains or channels the behavior of speakers of that language even in spheres which are not strictly linguistic. I will have occasion to speak of this hypothesis later, but here I want merely to point out that any psychological experiment which involves verbal behavior inevitably involves language as an implicit and (usually) unmanipulated independent variable. Not only is it nearly always unproved that the experimental results are *not* dependent on the language used, but it is also often the case that the experimenter is unaware of the necessity or the means of controlling stimulus variations which may be linguistically significant and hence may be significant sources of variance in his dependent variables. In the psychology of language we are dealing with a cultural system—a highly conventionalized, socially reinforced system which nearly every member of a culture acquires, in its essentials, at a relatively early age. If we are interested in processes of language acquisition our best course is to study very young children; there are several obvious complications if we study learners of second languages. There is plenty of work for us, nevertheless, in studying adult speakers of a language, as I shall mention in a moment.

Another special consideration affecting psycholinguistic methodology is the unique character of the linguistic system as a symbolic system capable of use in communication. Where the typical psychophysical experiment takes into account merely stimulus and sensation, or where the typical experiment in learning takes into account stimulus, organism, and response, the psycholinguistic experiment will involve in addition an intervening symbolic system.

A third consideration, which flows from the preceding, is that psycholinguistic methodology will perforce give more attention, at least initially, to the *content* of behavior than to the processes of behavior. By the time the psychologist gains access to the practiced native speaker of a language, which means any person of about age five or above, most of the linguistic system has been so well learned that we are left chiefly with the task of studying the properties of this system, or rather, the properties of the individual's behavior with respect to the system. The description of the linguistic system as such is for the most part the business of the linguistic scientist, who classifies and catalogs the distinctive sounds or phonemes of a language, its morphemes, its syntactical devices, and so forth. But all these things are important to the psychologist as well. One aspect of the linguistic system which is of particular importance to the psychologist is what is called meaning, especially since the linguist has been somewhat reluctant to come to terms with it. I hope I am not expected to say anything novel or startling about this much-discussed concept, but I will take the liberty of pointing out again that meaning has to do with certain relations between stimulus-situations and symbolic responses, and that the psychologist is presumably best-equipped to study such relations experimentally. The psychometric approaches to meaning developed by Mosier,[14] Osgood,[16] and Jones and Thurstone[11] would probably never have occurred to a linguist. The elucidation of linguistic meanings is fundamentally a matter of investigating the predictability of verbal behavior. Seen in this light, the task of psycholinguistics is essentially the same as that of all psychology: as Stevens phrases it,[21, p. 31] "... the complete definition of the stimulus to a given response involves the specification of all the transformations of the environment, both internal and external, that leave the response invariant." Let the stimuli or the responses, or both, be linguistic entities, and we have a tremendous range of problems in psycholinguistics.

The predictability of verbal behavior, that is, any behavior that involves linguistic entities in either the stimulus or the response side, or both, is a function chiefly of three conditions: (1) the rigorousness with which we can control stimulus contexts, including set, motivation, etc., as well as the more general physical and social environment; (2) the homogeneity of the speech community; and (3) the extent to which the individual has learned the code of his speech community. I am persuaded that verbal behavior is actually highly predictable, under appropriate conditions. The occasions when it appears capricious are chiefly occasions when it is difficult to control stimulus contexts—and this is true chiefly in those cases when the individual produces his own cues. We may hope to account for such seemingly capricious behavior by performing experiments in which *we* produce the cues.

Let me now adduce evidence from several small-scale pilot experiments on the predictability of verbal behavior.

The first result was obtained as a by-product of a project I am conducting on aptitude for foreign language learning. It has to do with the so-called picture-naming test originally devised by the Thurstones.[22] This test presents a series of line drawings of common objects and requires the subject, under speeded conditions, to write the first letter of the name of each object; the subject is told that any acceptable name will do. I wondered how consistently the objects were named, at least as indicated by the initial letters given. Analyzing the responses of a random sample of fifty West Point cadets to the first forty-nine items of the test, I found an average uncertainty (U) of only .564 bits, using Shannon's information measure.[20] This means that there was little disagreement on the names for these common objects. Items like flower, lamp, bicycle, foot, chair, drum, cat, banana, tree, and cow were named univocally; there was some disagreement about items like policeman (policeman or cop), airplane (airplane or plane), or even goose, often identified as a duck. The worst disagreement (with $U = 2.25$) was over a picture of a pair of rubber overshoes, where *B* (boots?), *S* (shoes?), *O* (overshoes?), and *G* (galoshes?) appeared among the responses. Here the unpredictability is probably due to the heterogeneity of the speech community—there being a number of terms for rubber overshoes used in different parts of the country or among different groups. Another type of disagreement came where the stimulus contained several elements, as where a picture of a chimney pouring forth smoke elicited both the responses *C* (chimney) and *S* (smoke?). The pictures, then, did not adequately control the subject's focus of attention. In a repetition of this experiment, an attempt should be made to construct the pictures so as to obtain a maximum of intersubject agreement in response, and insofar as the objects depicted represent a random sample of such objects, the resulting uncertainty figure could be regarded as a sort of baseline value for semantic uncertainty. There is considerable theoretical interest in the degree to which all features of the environment are univocally coded in a language system.

This experiment, simple as it is, is reminiscent of some recent work by Brown and Lenneberg,[4] who noted considerable *lack* of univocality in names which their subjects gave to color stimuli in English, and found evidence which promises that languages may differ in this respect. What is needed, therefore, is a systematic investigation of the univocality of coding, in different languages, of various aspects of the environment, including various natural phenomena, cultural objects and artifacts, kinship relations, and so on. One would suspect, for example, that cultural objects and artifacts are more univocally codable than natural phenomena. At any rate, only when such matters of content have been taken care of could we go on to investigate such matters of psychological process as response latency, rate of learning, warm-up effect, etc. We could find out, for example, whether Marbe's law, which states that the commonest responses are also the fastest, applies to the naming of stimuli as well as it does to free associations.

The study of the predictability of verbal behavior needs also to be extended systematically throughout the various categories of language structure. Charles C. Fries[7] shows how English structure is characterized by four main form classes (roughly, substantives, verbs, adjectives, and adverbs), plus a number of classes of what he calls "function words." The picture-naming experiment described above is concerned with agreement in coding stimuli which in English, at least, are generally expressed as nouns. We need information also on the codability of stimulus-situations which we generally express as verbs, adjectives, and adverbs. It would be interesting, for example, to make a linguistic analysis of the verbs which subjects use to describe the apparent behavior of the triangle and the circles which Heider and Simmel[9] depicted moving around in their animated-cartoon-like motion picture, and one could undoubtedly devise further experiments to narrow down the stimulus-symbol relationships.

THE ANTECEDENTS OF SENTENCE-SUBJECT

I have also been interested in the predictability of somewhat more complex and subtle aspects of verbal behavior. For example, in English sentences we have what is known as a subject and a predicate. In reporting any event the speaker must select some element of the situation and use it as the subject. Can we predict what element he will use as subjects? A related problem is the matter of active and passive verbs. Whether an active or a passive verb is used is usually contingent upon the selection of the subject. With the assistance of Mr. Michael Marge, I conducted an experiment

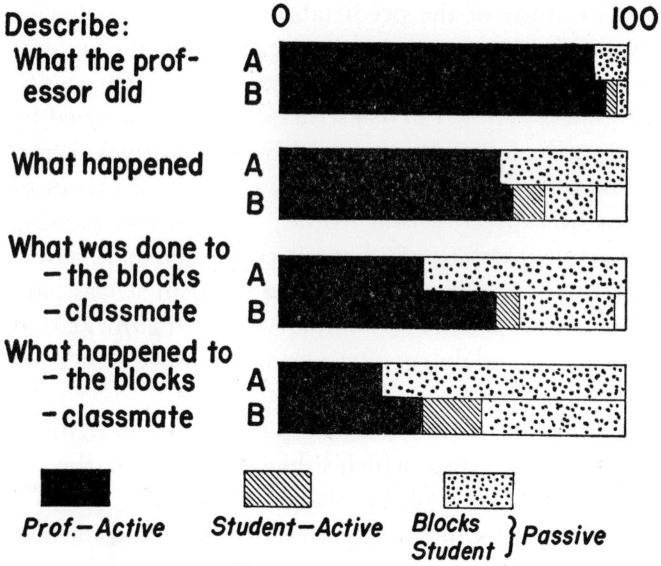

FIGURE 1. Incidence of subject-verb types used in response to two situations with four types of verbal cues.

involving 128 high school students. Seated in their classrooms, the students witnessed two brief action-situations which they were asked to describe "in a paragraph or two," in writing. The students were divided randomly in four groups, each group having a different verbal cue-stimulus printed on the papers on which they were to write their descriptions. The results are shown in Figure 1, which presents graphically the incidences of various subject-verb constructions used by the students. In each student's response, I counted only the *first* sentence used to describe an action. Now I myself must describe the two situations. Situation *A* was one in which Mr. Marge, who called himself "the professor," manipulated several colored blocks in a certain way—rearranging position, dropping them, etc. In this situation the two possible constructions were of the form: "Professor X'd the blocks" or "The blocks were X'd. . . ." Note the effect of the cue-stimuli on the relative incidence of these constructions. If you ask the students to describe "what the professor did," you get a high incidence of active constructions; decreasing frequency is noted with cues such as "Describe what happened," "Describe what was done to the blocks," and "Describe what happened to the blocks." The cue value of adding "to the blocks" to "what happened" in producing passive constructions is large and significant. Parallel results were obtained in Situation *B,* in which Mr. Marge acted out a little scene with a volunteer student, motioning to him to erase the blackboard and asking him to report to the principal when he refused. Here, in addition to the professor-active construction and the student-passive construction, we also find a student-active construction which has increasing frequency as we move from cue-stimulus 1 to 4. The problem now is to interpret these results. I think we are all happiest if we stick with objective statements about stimulus-response relationships, and these results show at least that we can to some extent control the selection of the sentence-subject. But can we go further? Can it be inferred from these results that the sentence-subject corresponds to some kind of perceptual organization—possibly the figural component of a figure-ground relation? Or do these results support Mowrer's contention[15] that the sentence-subject functions as a conditioned stimulus to the hearer? Or is the sentence-subject to be regarded as an interest-object? Whatever the case may be, it is clear that seemingly simple and innocent changes in verbal cues can result in considerable changes in verbal response.

The interpretation of sentence-subject is of possible practical importance, for example, in the interpretation of TAT protocols. I have studied the assignment of the *n (need)* and *p (press)* categories to the sentences of a TAT protocol reported by R. N. Sanford.[2, p. 570] The story is about a bandit who was put in jail and tried to get away. I find that a *need* category was assigned whenever *bandit* (or a grammatical equivalent) is the subject of a sentence with an active verb; a *press* category is assigned to sentences with *bandit* as the subject of a passive verb, or sentences with *they* (his captors) or other external objects as subjects of active verbs. In other words, the analysis can be done purely in linguistic terms. I don't know whether this reflects more the behavior of the thirteen-year-old girl who gave the TAT story or the behavior of the psychologist who did the analysis, but it is relevant to at least one of these. My point is that investigation of the antecedents of linguistic behaviors such as the selection of sentence-subject might aid in inferring something about the states of mind which give rise to verbal productions such as TAT protocols.

THE SEMANTICS OF SYNTAX

It is possible to explore even deeper in the realm of psychological syntax than this, and such explorations are necessary if we are to solve the problems which

Lashley[12, pp. 112-36] has recently posed. Lashley asks, essentially, by what mechanisms do we put together sentences? He rejects the notion of chain-reflexes but favors a theory of integrative sets. That is, sets or determining tendencies cued from different sources, as it were, are cerebrally integrated to produce a properly paced and structured utterance. What are some of these sets? I do not believe this question can be answered with confidence until we know more about the antecedents of certain things which we can, fortunately, observe in the end result of the speech process. I believe the proper place to start is with the highest order of structure that can be observed in the typical minimal utterance, that is, the sentence, because linguistically such structures precondition the pieces that can be fitted into them, and it seems reasonable to assume a corresponding psychological preconditioning. We can find an analogy in what we do when we decide to send a message to somebody in a distant city: before we compose the message we have to decide whether it is to be a formal letter, an informal note, a telegram, or perhaps even a poem, and this decision determines the kinds of verbal structures we use in our message.

What kinds of sentence-messages, or sentence-types, can we send when we speak or write? We learn in school grammar that there are declarative sentences, interrogative sentences, and imperative sentences, and this crude classification will serve for the moment. An unpublished pilot experiment conducted by Mr. Robert Plank and myself was designed to investigate the situational antecedents of these types, that is, the conditions of their elicitation. It was postulated initially that the effective variable is the speaker's perception of what we called the relative "information registry" of the speaker and his audience. That is, declarative sentences are normally uttered when the speaker perceives his own information as greater than that of his hearers. (I shall not consider such apparent exceptions as the pupil answering his teacher's questions.) Interrogative sentences result from the speaker's need for information or for material assistance. Commands result when the speaker perceives a particular kind of information, namely, the possibility of some action or some other instrumental behavior being under the control of the hearer. Our final results suggest that the situation is much more complex than this, but let me first describe our methodology.

We obtained our data by recording the verbal responses of pairs of subjects put in an experimental situation which was especially designed to elicit a variety of sentence structures by registering different kinds of information in each speaker at different times. Each pair was run separately, and the two subjects in each pair were seated opposite each other at a small table. An eye-height screen was placed across the middle of the table; each subject had, on his side of the screen, a set of objects which he was to manipulate, and a "script" containing the directions for each move in the "game," if it could be called a game, for there was absolutely no element of chance or competition. In addition, each S had a signal light which the experimenter, seated behind a one-way vision screen, used to pace the action. An example of a direction contained in the script is the following: "Proceed so that *your* CYLINDER will be on *his* GREEN peg." A more complicated example: *"If both his and your TOP-MIDDLE pegs are the SAME color,* put a CONE on yours; *if not,* put a CYLINDER on it." The subjects were trained in advance on what was meant by such terms as CONE and CYLINDER, for we were not interested in this type of semantic problem. Instead, we were interested in the sentence structure used by the subjects when they spoke, as they had to do in order to instruct each other, ask questions, get materials to pass to each other, and so on. The experiment involved, eventually, eight pairs of male graduate students, all native speakers of English. The analysis was based on the responses to twenty-two "directions" in the script, and upon the hearer's verbal responses to the speaker.

First I will deal with the primary verbal responses to the external situation as represented in the directions in the script and the particular arrangement of the subjects' pegs, blocks, and what not at any given stage. These directions were of six kinds; each kind varied only in respect to the particular forms, colors, or positions mentioned. It was also necessary to classify linguistically the structures of the speaker's responses; first into statements, questions, and commands, and then into subtypes of these. The criterion of classification was solely the pattern of linguistic form-classes involved in the structure of the response. For example, "Give me a yellow circle" and "Put that on your middle peg" would both be classed as imperatives. Having established these classes, we can set up an input-output

INPUT(FORM)	OUTPUT (FORM) STATEMENT: "I want your . . ." "This goes on . . ." 1	QUESTION: "Is your . . ." 2	QUESTION: "Do you have . . ." 3	QUESTION: "Will you please . . ." 4	QUESTION: "What color . . ." 5	IMPERATIVE: "Give me . . ." "Put this . . ." 6	
I. If his left-hand peg is green	—	8	—	—	—	—	8
II. If both his and your . . . are the same color	—	4	1	—	11	—	16
III. Give him a circle of the color of his bottom one	—	—	—	—	16	—	16
IV. Put a square on . . .	2	—	21	6	—	3	32
V. Proceed so that his . . . will be on your . . .	3	—	9	15	—	4	31
VI. Proceed so that your . . . will be on his . . .	5	—	8	11	—	54	78
	10	12	39	32	27	61	181

FIGURE 2. Frequencies of Sentence-Structure Types Used in Response to Six External-Situation Inputs.

matrix, as shown in Figure 2, which presents simply the frequencies. Let me point out the modal responses for each input. For Situation I, in which the directions stated a condition like "If his left-hand peg is green," the response was in every case what I call a binary-type question of the form "Is your left-hand peg green?" Situation II stated the condition in a different form, "If both his and your top pegs are of the same color . . . ," and the response was usually a multiple-condition question of the form "What's the color of your top peg" or "What color is your top peg?" but occasionally we find the binary-type question. Situation III, with a condition stated as "Give him a circle of the color of his bottom one," elicited always the multiple-condition question as described for Situation II. If we examine Situations I and III carefully, we can see the element which distinguishes them and probably results in the differential response. Both situations hinge upon the comparison of colors with a certain standard; in Situation I this standard is known to the speaker; in Situation III it is unknown. Now, in Situation III it is perfectly true that the speaker could run through the possibilities in succession, asking "Is it red? Is it green? Is it yellow?" etc., and this is perhaps the way some sort of computing machine would do it, as in Shannon's guessing game.[19] But it is more efficient, and our language provides a way to do it, to ask simply "What color is it" even in Situation I, but apparently we tend always to ask a binary question when we know a reference standard. In fact, a binary question might be said to betray a reference standard on the part of the speaker. Examine the responses to Situation II ("If both his and your top pages are the same color"); I suspect that those who used binary questions were the ones who checked the color of their own top peg before asking the question.

Let us pass on now to Situations IV, V, and VI, which never elicited binary or multiple-type questions of the kind found in Situations I, II, and III. In Situation IV, where the directions were of the form "Put a square on the blue peg," the needed object was always in the possession of the *other* subject. The modal response was a binary-type question of the form "Do you have a square?" This question could function either as a type of request (for some of the time the other subject promptly passed over a square), or as a true binary-type information question (for some of the time the other speaker said merely "Yes" and did nothing further). Perhaps the speaker really suspected that his partner really had no square, even though we carefully told the subjects there were no tricks. The other types of responses, though infrequent, were the out-and-out statement, "I want your . . .," the polite request, "Will you please give me . . .," and the imperative, "Give me." The social amenities are perhaps affecting these results; the accepted way of asking somebody for something, even though you know perfectly well he has it, is to ask him *whether* he has it. In Situation V ("Proceed so that *his* square will be on *your* green peg") the directions explicitly mention "*his* square," and while the modal response is the polite request-question, we still find some of the questions in the form "Do you have . . . ?" Situation VI happened to be well replicated in the experiment; the directions were of the form "Proceed so that *your* top piece will be on *his* RED peg." The modal response is the imperative, usually of the form "Put this on your red peg." Perhaps it is again a matter of social amenity: if you are telling someone to do something for *his* benefit, you use the imperative, but if it's for *your* benefit, you are more likely to use some sort of polite request.

To look back for a moment on Lashley's problem about the integration of syntactical elements, think how many conditions are thus demonstrated to affect the selection of sentence-type: (1) whether you need something from your partner or he needs it from you; (2) whether it's information or material assistance that is involved; (3) if it's information, whether you have a reference standard or not; (4) whether it's for your benefit or his; (5) whether you want to be nice and polite about it, on the one hand, or tough and efficient, on the other. This works out to twenty-four different combinations of conditions, and surely we have only scratched the surface in isolating such conditions. Furthermore, we have not considered the possible utterance, "I am wishing you would please tell me whether your middle peg is green or not," which seems to combine elements of statement, question, imperative, and politeness all rolled into one.

We also analyzed the second subject's verbal responses to the first subject. Fries[7] would call these "response utterance units" in contrast to "situation utterance units," and he finds many differences between the two types of units, notably in the fact that the "response utterance units" show less diversity of form. We set up another input-output matrix (Figure 3)

INPUT	OUTPUT Non-verbal	Yes-No	Con-firma-tion	Non-binary info	Echo state-ment	Echo ques-tion	Other
1. Statement	8	—	—	—	—	—	—
2. Binary question	—	11	1	—	—	—	—
3. Verify question	9	30	1	—	—	—	—
4. Polite request	35	10	—	—	1	1	—
5. Multiple question	—	—	—	24	—	3	1
6. Impera-tive	63	—	—	—	2	1	1

FIGURE 3. Incidence (frequencies) of response-types used by Speaker 2 in response to six types of verbal inputs used by Speaker 1. The inputs in this figure are the same as the outputs of Figure 2.

using the classes of Speaker A responses as the input and the classes of Speaker B responses, including nonverbal response, as the output. Again, the verbal behavior is highly predictable; indeed, the average conditional entropy is only .684 bits. Statements and commands elicit almost exclusively nonverbal responses. Binary questions of both kinds elicit the yes-no function class (including *surely, sure, O.K.,* and the like). Polite requests elicit nonverbal responses about three-quarters of the time. The multiple-condition question elicits chiefly a single word of the form-class specified by the question word (usually, here, the name of a color in response to "What color is . . ."). A few responses were what we call "echo questions" ("What color was it, did you say?") or "echo statements" ("Hm, you want a green one"), and there were miscellaneous other types of low frequency.

Obviously this experiment was only of an exploratory character; nevertheless, I believe the method could be fruitfully extended in many directions. First of all, it could be extended to more types of situations, with the hope of eliciting a greater variety of sentence-types and pin pointing the conditions of their elicitation. Secondly, one could begin to experiment with certain psychological processes which began to reveal themselves in this experiment. For example, we noted the tremendous influence of members of the pairs on each other in selecting speech styles. If one speaker chose one style of polite request, the other usually followed it. (For this and other reasons, it should be noted, the frequencies in our input-output tables are not completely independent.) There was one interesting sequence in which a certain speaker had led off with the statement-type command "This should go on your middle peg," in response to Situation VI. Similar phrases followed in the next three or four moves, also in Situation VI, but at one point the first speaker abbreviated to "orange peg." The other speaker, in the next move, then reverted to the straight imperative, "Put this on your red peg," which he had used in an earlier stage of the experiment. Apparently there is an extremely delicate balance between the alternative responses in certain sets, a balance which can easily be upset one way or the other by minimal cues.

LANGUAGE AND CONCEPTS

I have been struck with the fact that even the simple

situations and simple verbal responses involved in the experiments just described entail complex concepts. We have noted the elusiveness of the concept of sentence-subject and the intricacies of the conditions triggering different sentence-types. Much has been said by other writers on the relation between language and concepts, but I doubt that there has been any complete realization, on the part of most psychologists, of the extent of this relationship. As Sapir[18] made beautifully clear, linguistic concepts are contained not only in words but also in numerous grammatical devices such as suffixes and prefixes, syntactical arrangements, and the like. One may even claim that the phonemes of a language, that is, the distinctive elementary units of sound employed in the language, are concepts. Such a claim would be predicated on the definition of a concept as any habit of discriminatory behavior based either directly or mediately on discriminable features of the environment. It is easy to show, incidentally, that the phonemes of English correspond to learned habits of discrimination, and for this purpose I will show you one more input-output matrix (Figure 4). Certain English sounds, voiced and voiceless spirants, were presented by tape recording to a group of native speakers of English and to miscellaneous groups of foreigners who were just beginning to learn English. They were asked to identify the sounds; as may be seen by the table which gives the proportion of instances in which each input sound was identified as each of the six possible sounds, even the native speakers occasionally confused the sounds, but the foreign speakers made more errors.

		OUTPUT					
		s	z	θ	ð	f	v
s	N	.982	.009	—	—	—	—
	F	.852	.037	.074	.037	—	—
z	N	.090	.892	.009	—	—	—
	F	.049	.815	.037	.099	—	—
θ	N	.000	—	.712	.099	.180	—
	F	.037	—	.617	.037	.235	—
ð	N	—	.009	.099	.658	.018	.207
	F	—	.062	.136	.407	.037	.272
f	N	—	—	.027	.009	.937	.009
	F	—	—	.037	.012	.852	.037
v	N	—	—	—	.090	.018	.892
	F	—	.012	.025	.123	.012	.778

FIGURE 4. Input-Output Matrix Showing the Proportion of Times that Each of Six Consonants Was Identified as Each of the Six Consonants, by 37 Native Speakers of English (N) and 27 Foreigners (F) Just Beginning to Learn English.

To return, however, to our concept of a concept as a habit of discriminatory behavior based on discriminable features of the environment, let us note that our language provides a tremendous catalog of environmental distinctions. At some points it may appear crude and grossly indiscriminate; at other points it may be fantastically precise and delicate. One of the major tasks which each of us pursues in our life span is to learn the concepts provided by our language. Some of us may be just in the process of learning concepts like "entropy" and "complementarity," but of course we learned the great majority of linguistic concepts in childhood. There is something basically wrong when we psychologists continue to describe certain types of experiments as experiments in concept *formation* when they involve concepts which we can be sure were formed by the experimental subjects at much earlier ages. There can be no surer guarantee of this than the fact that in these experiments, for example, those of Heidbreder[8] or Bouthilet,[3] it is always possible to "give away" the solution verbally. As has already been suggested[13] we might better call them experiments in concept *evocation,* for that is what they are.

I would like to suggest, therefore, new directions in the study of concept evocation, and, for that matter, of problem solving, for most problem-solving situations involve concept evocation rather than the formation of new concepts. We should study concept evocation as dependent on the strength or latency of the concept in the individual's past experience, chiefly as indexed by language usage. Data from word counts, or better still, from tachistoscopic perception experiments, would provide reasonably good measures of verbal concept latency prior to the initiation of a training series. We would postulate that the rapidity or ease of concept evocation would be a direct function of initial concept latency. We would also postulate that the most difficult concepts to evoke, other things being equal, would be those which had never been formed, but to verify this hypothesis we would have to address ourselves to the almost impossible task of creating concepts which are *not* linguistically coded in the language, or at least not coded in terms of linguistic forms up through the compound word, let us say. Of course, we could also work with children young enough not to have acquired certain concepts. For example, with the assistance of Mr. Douglas Porter, I have started to work with methods of training children to identify structural elements (subjects, predicates, parts of speech, etc.) and have found that some children can very rapidly acquire these concepts at a much earlier age than might be supposed—that is, as early as the second or third grade. The case of grammatical concepts is an interesting one because in one sense the child has had to acquire and use concepts, unawares, in order to speak and understand the language at all; on the other hand, some children, and some adults, have difficulty in identifying grammatical entities at a conscious level of verbalization.

Early in this talk I mentioned the linguistic relativity hypothesis, having to do with the behavioral constraints presumably imposed by a particular language. Investigation of this hypothesis is likely to prove one of the most fruitful approaches to the whole field of cognition, for it will make necessary, as a prior step, a thoroughgoing examination of the role of linguistic processes in perception, discrimination, concept formation, concept evocation, and problem solving. That is, before we can compare the behavioral effects of different languages, we must investigate what kinds of linguistic phenomena produce given results in a given language. The various experiments reported in this paper are relevant to this problem as it pertains to English, and I am looking forward to performing some of these experiments with speakers of several American Indian languages. But I believe that experiments in concept evocation and problem solving offer an even more fruitful approach, since it is reasonable to postulate a mechanism whereby different degrees of availability of concepts, depending on the language spoken by the subject, might affect facility in concept evocation and problem solving.

There is, however, a premise in the above which at least needs to be mentioned. It is assumed by many, in particular by a number of linguistic scientists, that concepts are differentially available in different languages. This assumption has been made because language systems seem to differ so radically. Nevertheless, aside from scientific and technical concepts of recent origin, it is hard to find concepts which are not reportable in some way in any language we know of. Take the notion of reciprocity, for instance, epitomized in the phrase "each other" in English; you will find this concept, I believe, in every language we know of. Or take the notion of concomitant variation, encapsulated in English by the special syntactical construction "the more . . . , the more . . . ;" I doubt that you will find a language, however "primitive," which has no way of expressing this notion. Language universals according to the linguists Burt and Ethel Aginsky,[1] are important; language universals are traits found in every language. As a crude and perhaps hasty hypothesis, I would entertain the notion that any concept which can be handled by animals will also be found to be a language universal or composed of language universals. Obviously, animals recognize sex, and every language recognizes sex in some way. It is well known, too, that animals can learn to respond to alternative stimuli, and every language contains somewhere the notion of disjunction, "either . . . or . . . ."

Content, therefore, in the form of entities existing in linguistic codes and the concepts, perceptual organizations, discriminations, or what have you that correspond to these entities, is of major importance in psycholinguistics. I urge the intensive study and cataloging of content as I define it here. This will involve, I must warn you, not only psychological experiments of many kinds, but also a number of more or less purely linguistic explorations. Above all, it is one of the more urgent tasks of psycholinguistics.

REFERENCES

1. Aginsky, B., and Aginsky, E. The importance of language universals. *Word*, 1948, 4: 168-72.
2. Barker, R. G., Kounin, J. S., and Wright, H. F. *Child Behavior and Development*. New York: McGraw-Hill Book Co., 1943.
3. Bouthilet, L. "The Measurement of Intuitive Thinking." Ph.D. thesis, University of Chicago, 1948. [See reference 8, p. 745-46]
4. Brown, R. W., and Lenneberg, E. H. A study in language and cognition. *J. Abnorm. Soc. Psychol.*, 1954, 49: 454-62.
5. Carroll, J. B. (ed.). *Language, Thought, and Reality: Selected Writings of Benjamin Lee Whorf*. Cambridge, Mass.: The Technology Press, and New York: John Wiley & Sons, Inc. (in press).
6. ———. *The Study of Language*. Cambridge: Harvard University Press, 1953.
7. Fries, C. C. *The Structure of English*. New York: Harcourt, Brace & Co., 1952.
8. Heidbreder, E. An experimental study of thinking. *Arch. Psychol., N. Y.*, 1924, 11, No. 73.
9. Heider, F., and Simmel, M. An experimental study of apparent behavior. *Amer. J. Psychol.*, 1944, 57: 243-59.
10. Hoijer, Harry (ed.). *Language in Culture*. Chicago: University of Chicago Press, 1954.
11. Jones, L. V., and Thurstone, L. L. The psychophysics of semantics; an experimental investigation. *J. Applied Psychol.*, 1955, 39: 31-36.
12. Lashley, K. S. The problem of serial order in behavior. In Jeffress, L. A. (ed.). *Cerebral Mechanisms in Behavior*. New York: John Wiley & Sons, Inc., 1951.

13. Marks, M. R., and Ramond, C. K. A new technique for observing concept evocation. *J. Exp. Psychol.,* 1951, 42: 424-29.

14. Mosier, C. L. A psychometric study of meaning. *J. Soc. Psychol.,* 1941, 13:123-40.

15. Mowrer, O. H. The psychologist looks at language. *Amer. Psychologist,* 1954, 9: 660-94.

16. Osgood, C. E. The nature and measurement of meaning. *Psychol. Bull.,* 1952, 49:197-237.

17. Osgood, C. E., and Sebeok, T. A. (ed.). Psycholinguistics: a survey of theory and research problems. *Indiana University Publications in Anthropology and Linguistics,* Memoir 10, 1954. (Also issued as a supplement to *J. Abnorm. Soc. Psychol.,* Vol. 49, No. 4, 1954.)

18. Sapir, E. *Language.* New York: Henry Holt & Co., 1921.

19. Shannon, C. E. Prediction and entropy of printed English. *Bell Syst. Tech. J.,* 1951, 30: 50-64.

20. Shannon, C. E., and Weaver, W. *The Mathematical Theory of Communication.* Urbana: University of Illinois Press, 1949.

21. Stevens, S. S. (ed.). *Handbook of Experimental Psychology.* New York: John Wiley & Sons, Inc., 1951.

22. Thurstone, L. L., and Thurstone, T. G. Factorial studies of intelligence. *Psychometric Monographs,* 1938, No. 2.

SCIENTIFIC METHODOLOGY IN THE AREA OF PSYCHOTHERAPY

Roy M. Hamlin

THIS paper considers research methods in the area of psychotherapy. It mentions the techniques of psychotherapy as an applied "art" only incidentally.

In the area of psychotherapy, more attention than ever before is being given to scientific methodology. Therapists are gradually turning to scientific method as an absolute must for understanding what they are doing, and for evaluating the results. At the same time, psychologists trained in scientific method have shown increasing interest in submitting the problems of psychotherapy to careful scientific study.

The emerging current trend is a two-way trend, and has a two-way effect on the two aspects involved: (1) In spite of widespread pessimism to the contrary, the application of scientific scrutiny is altering practices in psychotherapy drastically. (2) In spite of widespread reactionary opinion to the contrary, the procedures of therapy, and knowledge gained therefrom, are altering the methods used by research psychologists in actual practice.

A host of developments illustrate the over-all trend. What are these developments, these subtrends, in scientific methodology in the area of psychotherapy? Four such trends, and three other pseudo-trends may be listed for consideration. The four trends are:

1. Objective consideration of therapy: the proce-

dures of psychotherapy are being exposed to scientific scrutiny.

2. Conceptualization: definitions, concepts, and principles are being energetically revised, discarded, sorted out, or reformulated.
3. Observation: although no one knows what to observe, the guide lines for observation are being questioned and revised. Specific new techniques of observation have not yet shown a mushroom development.
4. Analysis: methods of analysis, designs for relatively objective studies, are being developed, revived, or borrowed. More routine designs are being used in ways that might be specified.

The three pseudo-trends are:

1. Confusion: in this area, the research psychologists are running around like chickens with their heads off. This is the phenomenon Raimy so graphically reports in his 1952 *Annual Review* article.[1]
2. Paralysis: every attempt to start a specific planned study is open to criticism, and is usually sharply criticized. The criticisms are: *(a)* methodology is not rigorous enough; *(b)* methodology is not flexible enough, so that the study has no significance; and *(c)* the research worker lacks rigorous training either in science or in therapy.
3. Meager productivity: the output of significant objective studies is extremely thin.

Let us consider the first trend mentioned: the procedures of psychotherapy are being exposed to scientific scrutiny.

ROY M. HAMLIN

OBJECTIVE CONSIDERATION OF THERAPY

Eight years ago, in the first of these symposia on current trends, the speaker on psychotherapy, after one brief paragraph, took up the current trend which he had selected for first attention: The Objective Consideration of Therapy. In eight years, the over-all picture has changed markedly. Yet this same trend is still current and still deserves number one consideration.

You might suppose, in preparing a rabbit stew, that the first step is to skin the rabbit. This is not so. The first step is to catch the rabbit. In psychological science, we usually list as the first step: observe behavior. This is not the first step. The first step is to gain access to the behavior in order to observe it. This startling new addition to the traditional steps of scientific method has been made possible by procedures of psychotherapy.

The psychotherapist, for the better part of half a century, conducted his operations behind closed doors and in an atmosphere of mystery. Reports of what went on came from one source: the therapist. His verbal report and secondhand behavior were the only data which could possibly be observed. Even his report was often protected in another closed-door session with a control therapist. Scientific observation was out of the question. No unbiased observer was even considered. The possibility of two or more observers was regarded as equally absurd. Nothing was recorded at firsthand in reproducible form.[2]

Currently, the observation of therapy, *for research purposes,* presents an entirely different picture. Sound recordings, movies, one-way screens, and measures of physiological function expose for detailed scrutiny much that goes on. Mind-reading devices have not yet been developed, but should not be dismissed lightly as purely fanciful. The lie-detector concept, the use of "truth serums," the control scales in techniques like the MMPI, rigorous techniques employing selected judges to suggest: "When he said this, his verbal behavior really meant this." Such groping methods are not even adequate forerunners of what may be technically possible. The conscious and unconscious mind will be given operational and behavioral meaning, and their functioning will be recorded in reproducible form.

Mechanical devices, drugs, shorthand, and the like are not the only factors in the current development. Group therapy provides a situation in which several patients, and often several therapists, observe what is going on at firsthand. In some studies, patients take turns acting as therapists; they can influence what happens on the basis of their observations. Other studies claim that patients report material in the group situation which they do not report in individual contacts. The general trend toward some relaxation of the sanctified rules of secrecy is suggested by practices which allow a control therapist to sit in on a session when the immediate therapist seems to have reached a dead end. The possibility that a supervisory observer might learn something from a firsthand look at what's going on is revolutionary to many therapists. The objective scientist may not be impressed by the novelty of such a suggestion. The time may come when a second therapist may even communicate directly with the patient: the use of several therapists with one patient is being systematically, if not "scientifically," tried out. Formerly, every good therapist *knew* that recording of therapy ruined the true significance of the therapeutic relationship. He *knew* that the presence of a third person made any real progress impossible. And he *knew* that the therapy with groups could only be superficial and essentially didactic. This "knowledge" did not develop from observation. Even without carefully controlled studies, just a little firsthand observation has raised serious doubts about all this knowledge. Firsthand observation by more than one person is at least a step toward scientific method.

The most important element in this current trend is the attitude of leading thinkers who are accepted by psychotherapists as members of the in-group. These leaders of thought are usually trained both in psychotherapy and in research, but they are regarded as belonging to the psychotherapist "camp." Brief reference may be made to Western Psychiatric Institute, and to Dr. Brosin's multiple approach to a projected program of inculcating his psychiatric residents with some appreciation of scientific research methods. To be sure, Dr. Brosin hopes to develop some research psychiatrists; but he is also convinced that those who are never going to do anything but therapy must have some appreciation of scientific method. Especially at this stage of development, psychotherapists must be able to look on their own activities with a questioning and scientically critical eye. The reason they must be able to do so has perhaps been most trenchantly set forth by another psychotherapist, Glover, of the London Institute of Psycho-Analysis:

He [Glover] believes there has been an increasing tendency by psychoanalysts not to apply to their data such scientific controls as are available. He describes vividly how hearsay evidence becomes attested conclusion (given an analyst with seniority, enthusiasm or plain dogmatism); how a student whose professional career depends on overcoming "resistance" to the satisfaction of his training analyst can hardly be expected to defend his own scientific integrity against his analyst's theories and practice, so that inherent in the training situation is a tendency to perpetuate error; how, no matter how ideal their own analysis, individual analysts tend to show at meetings and elsewhere their own conflicts and "favorite pathological mechanisms"; how these three factors lead to the stereotyped proceedings of the Psycho-Analytical Association; and how peculiarly susceptible to fashion, "canalized no doubt through a hierarchy of transferences and countertransferences" are psychoanalytic groups. He has the impression that present-day psychoanalytic teaching preserves many of the disadvantages of mid-Victorian pedagogy and few of its advantages, and that the deficiencies of such authoritarian spoon-feeding are not remedied, as is often thought, by the candidate's training analysis. He believes it is time these issues were faced, and that a first task of psychoanalysts is to settle down to the arduous task of defining terms, verifying criteria, and developing reliable statistics. His portrayal of the association between lack of scientific productivity and the psychoanalytic training procedure is that of a self-reinforcing system with tremendous internal resistance to change.[3]

The most striking feature of this first current trend is the attitude among leading therapists—like Brosin, Glover, and many, many more. They are now the most outspoken advocates of scientific method. The situation has changed markedly since eight years ago, when Rogers saw himself as standing almost alone in sticking out his neck for honest science.

CONCEPTUALIZATION

The first step in the scientific study of psychotherapy is to gain access to the behavior under consideration. The second current trend concerns the meaning of words. Definitions, concepts, and stated principles are being energetically revised, discarded, sorted out, or reformulated.

The psychotherapist has long tended to describe behavior in terms that are loaded with connotations, analogies, intuitions, phraseology resembling that of the novelist or poet, feeling tones. Figures of speech, like the Oedipus complex, never entirely shake off the vague illogic of their dream world origin. Words like "mothering" and phrases like "returning to the womb" still hold a wavering but strategic position somewhere between dream-thinking and meaningful concepts.

The experimentalist has a different approach to the definition of terms. He compresses meaning to a minimum, preferably to a point where it can be represented in a relatively simple operation. The procedure resembles the practices of the South American headhunters. These businesslike South American students of man first remove the man's head, a process which has some effect on the real-life significance of the subject. They then extract the blood and other lifelike fluids, and compress the head gradually to a convenient size. In this miniature and dehydrated form, the head can be much more readily filed away on a shelf. The scientist's use of words does indeed carry with it some of the same disadvantages. Yet without such reduction the greatest value of words is never fully realized. At least some scientific words must ultimately represent a precisely parallel correlate in objective reality.

The current trend among molders of thought who are psychotherapists is to review every concept, every term, and every verbally expressed principle in the light of scientific rules. We find an entire book written on the concept of transference. This book, written on a single word, is only an illustration of the trend. It is one example of a whole series of books and articles which include contributions by Clara Thompson, Fromm-Reichman, and others. The Harry Stack Sullivan group has gradually moved toward verbal patterns that bring them closer and closer to the rules of research psychology.

This particular book, Wolstein's *Transference,* is a good illustration of the trend for several reasons. The author has formal training in scientific method, in philosophy, and in psychotherapy. His primary identification is with a group of psychotherapists; yet he is willing to question dictums, and to attack authoritarianism as a basis for accepting principles. Specifically, he is more harsh in his criticisms than the authors of the second illustrative book, which will be cited shortly and which represents the same trend from the research psychologists' approach. Finally, his method throughout is from the standpoint of operationalism. The complete success of his attempt need not be considered, since the trend continues.

Briefly, Wolstein suggests that transference refers

first of all to behavior observed right here and right now: to behavior observable at firsthand, as it takes place with two people present. It is from this definition and from this priority of here-and-now observation, that the word must take its basic meaning. Previous patterns of behavior, including memory-extrapolated infant patterns, are not excluded from consideration, but the word is anchored primarily to specified immediate observations.

A second book illustrates the same emphasis on definitions and concepts. Again, this second book is a good illustration of the current trend for several reasons. Wolstein's book has a history, and fits into a context, in terms of the Sullivan group of psychotherapy. Dollard and Miller's book, *Personality and Psychotherapy,* has a history and context related to research psychology and experimental learning theory. Hull's theories, Miller's studies of conflict dating back fifteen years or so, Sears' experiments and review of objective studies of psychoanalytic concepts might be mentioned. As with Wolstein's book, here again we have authors trained in scientific method, in theory, and in psychotherapy. Wolstein, writing in his role as a therapist, is harsh in his attacks on long-accepted concepts. Dollard and Miller, writing as research-trained psychologists, lean over backwards to retain or find maximum scientific virtue in concepts developing from the practice of psychotherapy.

Dollard and Miller's book need not be evaluated here in all its aspects, but its major purpose is an attempt to integrate terms from psychoanalysis and from learning theory. It is a sort of English-French, French-

English dictionary. Certainly, it is more than this: the terms change, are integrated, are added to. They draw new meaning from the two combined backgrounds of study. Incidentally, Dollard and Miller devote a chapter to parallel Wolstein's book on transference, and relate the term to generalization and similar learning theory concepts. The main focus of the book is clear: it is a systematic comparative review of terms, concepts, verbally expressed principles. This comparative method is somewhat like that of Ford and Beach in their book on sexual behavior, where they integrate animal studies, cultural studies, and experimental studies. Information from nonexperimental sources is not automatically ignored as nonscientific. This integrating procedure is, of course, part of scientific method; and is an important current trend.

The systematic study of terms and principles is only part of the current trend in conceptualization. For example, Saslow writes: "Review of studies (since 1943) of the process of client centered therapy leads to the inference that they have been mainly studies in conceptualization; they have helped build ways of looking at therapy which have added to the theory-building process."[4] The rash of theory building over the past fifteen years, which has now subsided into some perspective, was influenced to a marked degree by practices in psychotherapy. This relationship cannot be briefly substantiated, but two points are familiar enough: (1) the widely repeated claim that the only over-all theory of personality was psychoanalysis, and (2) the practice in therapy of working very freely in terms of assumptions that ran far ahead of the data.

The effect on present research attitudes toward hypothetico-deductive approaches; the effect on greater tolerance toward unreduced, dreamlike, or intuitive terms as possibly representing a step in science; and the effect on the developing studies of creativity are all related. The over-all trend in conceptualization is too complex to be summarized. It is a major trend and has only been cited and illustrated here.

OBSERVATION

The data of psychotherapy are being made available for scientific study. Concepts and terms are being thoroughly scrutinized. The third current trend is related to observation. Research psychologists are flabbergasted by the problem of what to observe and how to observe.

Techniques are clumsy, inadequate, and "peripheral." The research psychologist has failed to capitalize on the procedures of psychotherapy. He has failed to select and adopt therapy procedures—to reduce them to clear-cut, controlled methods. He feels that his traditional methods are inadequate to deal with real-life problems. For example, he is uneasily reluctant to attack any problem which *suggests* events "remote" in time or observability (such as infant memories); any data which are "remote" in complexity (multivariable behavior or broad life patterns); any data which are "remote" in meaning (where manifest content has to be translated into latent content); and any data which are "remote" in frequency of occurrence (idiographic or unique individual behavior).

These categories of behavior are "remote" because

of timid, clumsy methods of observation. The techniques so far developed fail to come to grips with the basic units or variables which are now available for observation. The behavior is here and now, real-life behavior right before our eyes. It is "remote" because of poor observation. The five blind men, each feeling a different part of the elephant, could not build up a picture of the real-life elephant. They needed eyes to see what was obviously there.

In this situation, one tendency is to observe everything and record everything, wholesale and indiscriminately, with no rationale and no selectivity. Six months of therapy at the rate of several hours a week are tape recorded word for word. Tape has been developed in two-track form, so that running comments as voluminous as the original material can be recorded also. Four-lane highways may be anticipated, to provide for a mother commentator, a father commentator, and a peer commentator, as well as the subject. This trend represents democracy at work. Whole books are written on material from one subject. In the over-all picture, these are paralleled by a book on fourteen hours in the life of one seven-year-old boy.

This trend in observation and recording is certainly a welcome development after the dark ages of therapeutic secrecy. Like a young child who suddenly finds himself able to observe and manipulate his environment, the psychologist may seem to go to extremes. The child wants to observe everything for the sake of observing, manipulate everything, and discover what it takes to break or ruin everything.

The value of the trend has limits, of course. The

physicist, Ampere, believed he could predict anything if he knew the location and velocity of every molecule. On a psychological level, some such faith is implied in the current emphasis on observation. In psychopathology, Pinel long ago made an important advance by insisting that careful records be kept on patients. Under the influence of Adolph Meyer, these records grew in size until they threatened to outweigh the patient in sheer bulk and overshadow the patient in complexity and wealth of detail.

Nevertheless, two illustrations may be cited to suggest important elements in the current development that are a definite advance. Dollard, Auld, and White's *Steps in Psychotherapy* may slip by the censor of psychological methodology as a sort of case-study illustration and teaching manual. On the other hand, it may be accepted as an illustration of a research method. It is a study of one individual case in a setting of broad research background and a framework of theory. It is not an experiment of proof. The book by Barker and Wright on *One Boy's Day* is a similar example closely related to the problems of therapy. It is part of a planned approach, and shows evidences of a considered methodology. It is not anecdotal or a study of a unique event.

One neurotic block, the absurd misunderstanding of the unique event concept, may gradually fall into perspective. Research psychologists will no longer close their eyes to data which are "remote" in frequency of occurrence. Eventually, of course, cross comparisons may be made with numerous studies. The cross-cultural comparisons of Yale anthropologists should suggest guidelines. Comparisons of repeated behaviors within the individual are possible. The recent studies of Ebbinghaus (1882) may serve as a tentative model. The method of idiographic studies has not been firmly set forth in psychology and will not be attempted here.

There is some indication that research psychologists are moving their techniques of observation and analysis a little closer to the behavioral data of psychotherapy. The first task was to gain access to the data; progress in this task is well under way. The second task is for the research psychologist to open his eyes, to adopt or develop methods for dealing with the data as it actually presents itself. This second task involves conceptualization, observation, and analysis. Some further current tendencies may be considered under the heading of analysis.

ANALYSIS

As a fourth current trend, methods of analysis, designs for relatively objective studies, are being developed. As illustrations, some of Cronbach's work, the use of self-sorts or Q-sorts, and the critical incident technique of that well-known analyst, Dr. John C. Flanagan, suggest specific points of interest, not necessarily as the most representative of what is actually being done in the area of psychotherapy.

Previously, I listed examples of certain behavioral data which are "remote" from the research psychologist because of his rigidity in clinging to clumsy techniques. The seance room of the psychotherapist has been opened up for scientific inspection. The research psychologist must leave his "brass instruments" and come out of his ivory tower. In the first Current Trends conference, eight years ago, Rogers stated: "The struggle to develop appropriate research procedures will be, in all probability, one of the significant future trends." At least the *struggle* and the beginnings of the trend are evident now, eight years later.

With a huge mass of verbal behavior recorded on a series of therapy interviews, what does the research psychologist select to observe? He counts nouns, adjectives, and adverbs. He counts total number of words and number of different words used (Roshal). He is not "mentalistic." He studies behavior. Roshal's study is a good study; it represents progress. First, some meaning is given to this peripheral approach by a legitimate proposition: successful therapy should increase variability of behavior, and *even* variety of noises made might reflect this change. Second, the study is only one in a planned shotgun approach. And third, it points up the shortcomings in observational techniques.[5]

The Distress-Relief Quotient and Raimy's sorting of phrases into favorable and unfavorable self-attitudes were ingenious innovations ten years ago, but must be classified as examples of arrested progress now. For the most part, the use of such formalized techniques as the Rorschach and MMPI, to reflect and delineate therapy process, is not much of an advance. Most of the techniques so far developed fail to come to grips with the basic units or variables that are now available for observation. There is great need for "thinking in other categories." The data of psychotherapy are right in front of our eyes, but our methods of observation and analysis are remote from the data. The examples listed before may be repeated. We have difficulty observing (1) verbal behavior suggesting memories, (2) multivariable and broad pattern behavior, (3) verbal behavior freed from manifest meaning, and (4) individual behavior.

To state the difficulty another way, we have great difficulty observing patient or real-life oriented behavior. It is easier to observe instrument oriented behavior.

Two illustrations suggested some trend to move methodology closer to the scientific study of data "remote" in frequency of occurrence. The research psychologist's mentalistic concept of a unique event is gradually giving way. That the multitude of behaviors displayed by one individual constituted a nonscientific unique event was never true in observed reality.

Cronbach's varied approaches constitute the most sophisticated and realistic attempt to bring techniques closer to multivariable behavior. The answer (not necessarily Cronbach's answer) seems to be in conceptualizing, deriving, and establishing on a firm basis new units of behavior, broad patterns of behavior which can be handled as single variables or as a small number of variables. This idea in itself is certainly not new. The current trend is to develop a clear-cut scientific method to establish such variables in the areas related to psychotherapy.

Flanagan's critical incident has hardly been tried out in the area of psychotherapy. In one respect, it is not an ideal illustration of the current trend. It relies on a very small fragment of behavior from a large number of subjects. However, it has other features in line with the trend. In the first place, it is a clearly set forth method. Second, it is so little experiment-bound in conception that it is regarded as dubiously suitable for graduate student theses. Third, it handles units of *verbal* behavior as classifiable units of behavior, even though the actual incident reports are simply loaded with subjective opinion, interpretation of motives, and mentalistic concepts. In a perfectly legitimate formulation, he has sure slipped one past the experimentalist censor in this technique. Fourth, the units of verbal behavior retain a sufficient degree of broad pattern complexity. The technique approaches real-life behavior. And, finally, the behavior observed is, to a high degree, subject-centered. It is not entirely imposed on the subject by the recording procedures.

Dr. Flanagan is now asking teachers to report critical incidents of good behavior and of bad behavior in school children. (Example: Johnny poured soup down the vice principal's neck in the cafeteria.) He then asks them what should be done to reinforce or stamp out such behavior. (Example: teachers' salaries should be raised.) This technique comes to grips with the basic problems of psychotherapy.

In spite of many shortcomings and difficulties, the so-called Q-sort technique or self-sort opens up many possibilities. It is a crude and minimal way of translating manifest behavior into "latent" content. It is idiographic. It is partially subject-oriented rather than technique-oriented. It avoids many of the criticisms in the current reactionary trend against projective techniques. (The true projective technique allows the subject to give a subject-oriented response, or as Cattell says, an "imaginative" response. The significant antecedent conditions are minimally determined by the technique. The methodological problem is the same as in psychotherapy, and the extension or adaptation of methods to go as far as possible in recording such real-life behavior meaningfully should not be lightly abandoned.) Finally, it has a history in statistics specifically associated with problems of psychotherapy.

Self-concept, self-ideal concept are replaced by observed behavior. A self-sort before therapy can be correlated with a self-sort after therapy, with a self-ideal sort, etc. The possibilities have hardly been touched yet. Items taken entirely from the therapy problems of one category of subject can be sorted by other subjects. Therapy problem, plan, process, and outcome may be clarified and sorted out for different patients. Essentially, the technique is cited here as one indication that methods can be brought closer to behavior that is related to the fact that man talks, uses symbols, and perceives in terms of past, symbolically recorded events.

PSEUDO-TRENDS

Three pseudo-trends or phenomena were listed earlier: confusion, paralysis, and meager output of significant "objective" research. There is reason to note all three phenomena, but they may now be regarded as secondary phenomena, which somewhat observe the over-all development rather than represent it.

The confusion at present is chiefly apparent in two

respects. The over-all progress is certainly not clear to any one person. I have attempted a rough formulation, but it will surely turn out to be inadequate in many features. Second, the development of methods of observation and analysis is associated with confusion of a specific sort: tentative methods are used which have not been widely used in research psychology recently. However, these methods for the most part are not clearly formulated and set forth. This situation leads to an impression of unscientific confusion.

The impression of paralysis is associated with indecision about selecting a method, or settling on an inadequate formulation of the method, once selected. The apparent paralysis is also associated with stubborn reactionary criticism and lack of acceptance of what is being done. As one trend that is about to become apparent, the impression of paralysis may be confidently expected to evaporate. The client-centered research is not paralyzed. Nor is Mowrer, Miller, and Dollard, research in the area of psychosomatic disorders and stress diseases, epidemiological approaches, critical incident studies, Barker and Wright's and similar related approaches, B. F. Skinner in his invasion of catatonic behavior, Cronbach and similar approaches, studies of alcoholism, other broad multiple facet developments, to suggest only a few examples.

The impression of meager output of "objective" studies is only partly justified. The general trends are not reflected adequately in APA journals, because they are too reactionary. In his 1952 *Annual Review* survey, Raimy had to stress books rather than journal articles. In his parallel 1955 survey, Meehl limited his consideration largely to "objective" studies that paralleled closely final-step experiments of proof, preferably meeting rigid standards. The impression of meager output is partially due to experiment-bound thinking that is much too narrow in its interpretation of objective science. Research psychologists are so experiment-bound that they make it difficult for themselves to carry out sound experiments, and to develop a sound experimental science.

CONCLUSION

This discussion has been limited to current trends in scientific methodology in the area of psychotherapy. The methods of psychotherapy as an applied technique have not been considered, except as they are gradually coming under the scrutiny of scientific observation, or are being modified by the developing interest in scientific analysis and validation.

The major complex of trends which have been considered are all closely interrelated and, in a general way, might even be considered one over-all trend. Psychological therapists and research-trained psychologists are making a tremendous effort to reconcile their approaches into one over-all approach. The problem of establishing transition between the observational methods of therapy and the observational methods of science is a difficult problem, but also a poorly formulated one. It is difficult to see clearly what the problem is. The difficulty accounts in large part for the impression of confusion, of hectic activity without clear direction, referred to by Raimy; for the impression of paralysis and meager productivity of "objective" research.

The apparent confusion, disagreements, paralysis, and lack of significant directed progress in research I have chosen to dismiss as pseudo-trends, without real importance. (It is easy for me to do this. On more than one occasion, my analyst used to predict that I would come in some day, talk quietly for half an hour about my mentalistic problems, and then remark casually: "Oh, by the way, my house burnt down this morning." On these occasions, he was usually tearing his unconscious hair in frustration with me, and no independent, unbiased observer was present to confirm his report of my actual behavior. Furthermore, my house never did burn down.)

Be that as it may, the impression that the current trend is a vigorous movement in fifty different directions at the same time should not be misleading. The uncertainty, the waste effort, the false starts and random movements do not mean that the trend is not, in general, moving toward, or evolving, a goal. The hectic behavior is like that of a child trying for the first time to reach an object. Eventually, the reaching movement becomes efficient, "automatic," and seems extremely simple. In the earlier fumbling process, considerable frustration and flares of misdirected anger are usually observed.

The trends suggested today were roughly foreshadowed in the presentation on current trends in psychotherapy eight years ago. The first heading considered today is the same one given first consideration eight years ago; from an early draft, I altered the heading slightly to match precisely the one used eight years ago: The Objective Consideration of Therapy. Similarly, the presentation eight years ago set the stage, in a peculiarly pertinent sentence, for the discussion of research methodology in this area today: "The struggle to develop appropriate research procedures will be, in all probability, one of the significant future trends." The future of eight years ago is with us today; the struggle is centered in the attempt to develop research methods. In the intervening years, the task has clarified somewhat, and broken down into the three other trends listed: (1) conceptualization—building general frameworks to help look at therapy; (2) actual techniques of observation; and (3) techniques for analyzing the observed data, for effecting the integration of conceptualization and recorded behavior.

If the first current trend considered eight years ago was making the data of psychotherapy available for observation, in what sense is this still a current trend now? The situation has altered markedly and the trend still continues. One aspect in particular is strikingly different: this aspect is the attitude of leaders among psychological therapists of all schools. Now, the leaders of thought among therapists are among the strongest advocates of the need for scientific scrutiny; the severest critics of their own concepts, of their closed system of thinking, of their acceptance of principles on the basis of authority and tradition. The Sullivan group has set out to pull apart and revise every major sanctified principle. The quotation from Glover sounds like the confession of an ex-Russian premier just before he is taken out to be shot. The insistence among leading therapists on the necessity of indoctrinating therapy students in scientific patterns of thought increases. In more recent writings research psychologists sound like apologists for traditional psychotherapy, rather than like the opposition. The situation has changed in the past eight years.

The therapist is coming out of his mystery-shrouded seance room. As yet, the intransigent research psychologist has not shown comparable progress in leaving his "brass instruments" and in coming out of his "ivory tower." This is not intended as an invidious comparison. It is not because many therapists have been analyzed and are therefore better adjusted. It is simply a matter of the pattern of development, a question of timing. If the research psychologist came out without his brass instruments now, he wouldn't have any pants on at all. He doesn't have anything else to wear.

In the light of the current developments suggested, this is no longer strictly true, of course. He could come out disguised as a critical incident, or in a Q-sort of outfit, or in some costume that looked perfectly idiographic.

With the behavioral data available for observation, the widespread interest in conceptualization was listed as the second current trend. Recognizing the many other influences involved, the impact of concepts and principles derived from therapy played an important part in the intense interest in theory building. The willingness to accept an unusually free employment of hypothetico-deductive approaches is, in part, a compromise with psychotherapeutic "mentalism." The current trend was illustrated only, by one example of the questioning of concepts from the Sullivanian series, and by Dollard and Miller's book attempting to integrate analytic and learning theory concepts. Saslow's suggestion that client-centered research has been concerned chiefly with conceptualization was simply quoted.

The third current trend suggested here concerned specific methods of observation. Mechanical devices and the like were emphasized eight years ago and have, of course, developed since then. Attempts to bring observational methods closer to real-life behavior are gradually emerging. Many aspects of significant behavior are "remote" only in the sense that available techniques are clumsy. The research psychologist is specifically hesitant to observe or even admit the existence of: (1) verbal behavior suggesting memories; (2) multivariable and broad pattern behavior; (3) verbal behavior freed from manifest meaning; (4) individual behavior; and (5) subject determined behavior. Two examples of relatively sound studies of single subjects were cited: Barker and Wright, and Miller and Dollard. Similar developments were illustrated in terms of the fourth trend analysis. Cronbach, Flanagan, and Q-sort were mentioned.

The major current trend is a willingness to observe behavior formerly shunned, to observe this behavior in new ways, and to work toward new classifications of emergent variables. There is no trend toward mentalism, toward unobservable events as the basic data of psychology; on the contrary, there is less danger of such a trend than ever before. The trend is toward more comprehensive immediate observation and toward an all-out attempt to employ every means to understand or classify these observations into significant units or variables. The research psychologist is systematically reviewing and revising his techniques, concepts, and accumulated knowledge in line with these trends. To a degree, certainly, he is abandoning the expectation of major insights developing magically from exhaustive gathering and manipulation of petty facts. Experimentation must parallel the significant realities of psychological behavior. New research methods of observation, classification, and analysis are gradually developing. The impetus for these trends has come, to an important degree, from the procedures of psychotherapy and from the felt need to analyze and evaluate psychotherapy in a thorough-going, scientific fashion.

REFERENCES

1. Raimy is, of course, simply emphasizing the difficulty of identifying significant trends in a situation which he describes as follows: "The field of psychotherapy appears to have an enormous but somewhat leaderless vitality. Research plays little part; theory is largely at the clinical level; and speculation as to underlying principles and relevant factors reigns supreme. Description of methods of treatment are largely confined to anecdotal presentations or discussions of presumed principles conducted at a considerable distance from the operational sphere. Finally, thousands and thousands of persons are being treated in one fashion or another, but no one seems very certain what the outcome has been or will be." *(Annual Review of Psychology,* 1952, p. 321.) This quotation summarizes well the main points stressed by various psychologists. These phenomena are "pseudo-trends" in the sense that, even if they represent the present situation accurately, they can hardly be expected to thrive indefinitely under scientific scrutiny.

2. In addition to the audience who heard this paper given, several critics read it and made comments. The above paragraph was condemned vigorously by some, presumably as reflecting abysmal ignorance of, or stubborn failure to appreciate, much that has been done in the period referred to, with intentional vagueness, as "the better part of half a century." The author has noted this criticism, but has allowed the paragraph to stand as written, in conjunction with the rest of the section, which should clarify the intent to some extent. In a brief overview, the paragraph may suggest some knowledge and appreciation of much that has *not been done.* Incidentally, it has been amusing to note the almost precise point in the paper, where one camp of critics ceases to express strong resentment and starts to applaud, and the other camp ceases to applaud and starts to object violently.
3. The paraphrase of Glover's criticisms is quoted from Saslow, *Annual Review of Psychology,* 1954, p. 333.
4. *Annual Review of Psychology,* 1954, p. 312.
5. Roshal's study is one of the interesting collection of related Ph.D. dissertations assembled in summary form by W. U. Snyder: *Group Report of a Program of Research in Psychotherapy.*

GUILT, SHAME, AND OTHER REACTIVE MOTIVES

THOMAS M. FRENCH

IT is now generally recognized that neuroses are reactions to unconscious conflicts. In order to understand an unconscious conflict we should distinguish two kinds of motives—a "disturbing motive," which has usually been repressed, and a "reactive motive," which is responsible for the disturbing motive's having been repressed.

Psychoanalysts were at first interested chiefly in disturbing motives. The patient's struggle to keep these disturbing motives repressed was usually called "resistance," but the motives for resistance were often not carefully analyzed. Sometimes resistance was attributed to a psychic "censor," but little attempt was made to analyze the "reactive" motives that had inspired the censorship.

Still, in order to understand a neurosis or a patient's personality structure, we should know both of the motives that are involved in an underlying conflict. When we are interested in the functioning of the personality as a whole, *the motives that inspire the censorship are just as important* to discover *as the motives that are repressed.* We should try to find out not only the patient's disturbing motive but also the "reactive motive" that has caused him to repress, or to inhibit, or to try to explain away his "disturbing motive."

In this paper I shall try to distinguish a number of

different kinds of reactive motives. Since Freud published *The Ego and the Id,* psychoanalysts have been much interested in reactions to guilt, but the word "guilt" is often used loosely to include many other kinds of reactions. For example, guilt should be distinguished from fear of loss of a parent's love, from fear of punishment, and from shame.

As a basis for understanding the distinction between guilt and fear of loss of love we recapitulate Freud's two successive attempts to explain how the conscience is formed in the course of a child's development. The first of Freud's reconstructions was part of his elaboration of the concept of narcissism. One form of infantile narcissism is a kind of megalomania: the infant likes to imagine himself omnipotent and perfect. Yet his actual helplessness and the criticisms of his parents make it impossible for him to maintain this illusion. He protects himself from disillusionment by attributing the wished-for perfection to an Ego-ideal. The conscience arises as a need to achieve this ideal in reality.

Later, supplementing this account, Freud (1923) derived the conscience from the child's attempts to resolve the Oedipus complex. In the Oedipus complex the little boy's ambition to be powerful like the father fuses with his desire to possess the mother sexually. Thwarted in this desire by his fear of castration by the father, he is driven to seek another way of identifying with the father's power. He achieves this goal by imposing on himself the father's prohibitions, threats, and punishments. The part of the personality that splits off thus to identify with the father's prohibitive role is the conscience or Superego. Sometimes we describe this process by saying that the Superego arises by "introjection" of the father's prohibitive role.

The inverted Oedipus complex also contributes to the formation of the Superego, since the little boy is thwarted also in his desire to be loved sexually by the father. When the Superego takes over the father's role, submitting to the restraints and punishments imposed by the Superego can serve as a substitute for gratification of the boy's feminine desire to submit to the father.

Guilt and Fear of Loss of Love. By means of this reconstruction we can now distinguish between guilt and fear of loss of a parent's love. In an early paper (1928), Anna Freud insisted on the importance of this distinction as a basis for understanding the differences between child analysis and the analysis of adult patients. She called attention to the fact that the child's Superego can usually not be counted on to inhibit disturbing impulses unless it is supported by prohibitions from the parents or from the analyst. In children the process of introjecting parental prohibitions has usually not been completed; and the prohibitions imposed by the Superego must therefore be re-enforced either by fear of punishment or by fear of loss of the parents' love.

The same distinction between guilt and fear of loss of love as reactive motives is also important sometimes in order to understand adult patients. In these patients, too, the process of introjection of parental inhibitions has been incomplete; and fear of loss of love is often the dominant inhibitory motive, supplementing or even replacing guilt. This distinction may be important in determining what symptom a patient will develop at a particular time. For example, in our studies (1941) of bronchial asthma at the Chicago Psychoanalytic Institute, we found that asthma attacks are precipitated only by situations in which fear of estrangement (or separation) from a mother figure is the inhibiting motive. During periods when introjection of parental prohibitions was more successful, the patients developed other symptoms, such as neurotic compulsions, but were free of asthma. In other words, at such time the patient's conscience, which caused him to condemn himself, served as a kind of buffer, protecting him from the danger of offending a mother figure, which might otherwise have precipitated an asthma attack.

Guilt and Inferiority Feelings. Another distinction that is important for understanding the behavior of patients is the distinction between guilt and feelings of inferiority or shame. Alexander (1935) pointed out, for example, that feelings of inferiority on account of strong dependent needs are often reacted to with aggressive criminal behavior; the criminal is trying to prove that he is not soft but tough. Later (1938), Alexander called attention to the fact that such feelings of inferiority often come into direct conflict with guilt feelings. In inhibited and compulsive characters this alternation between guilt and feelings of inferiority may be exceedingly disabling. The patient's guilt inhibits the patient's aggressive impulses and subdues a man into submissive attitudes, but his pride will not permit him to accept his submissive attitudes, and gives rise to feelings of inferiority, which tend to drive him again into aggressive behavior.

More recently, Piers (1953) has elaborated this contrast further, insisting on the distinction between guilt and shame. The word "shame," which he uses in a somewhat broader sense than usual, corresponds to Alexander's "feelings of inferiority." Piers finds the essential difference between guilt and shame in the fact that guilt inhibits and condemns transgression whereas shame demands achievement of a positive goal. He relates this contrast between shame and guilt to Freud's two earlier terms for the conscience. Shame, when its goal is positive achievement, he thinks of as a reaction to the Ego ideal; whereas guilt, he believes, proceeds from the Superego.

Further Classification of Reactive Motives. The distinctions between guilt and fear of loss of love and between guilt and inferiority feelings do not anywhere near exhaust the possible variations in a patient's reactive motives. Indeed, each of the kinds of reactive motive that we have enumerated should be classified further into subgroups.

An important distinction is one between the negative and positive goals of a reactive motive. For example, feelings of inferiority and shame are uncomfortable or disturbing feelings of which a person tries to rid himself by compensatory behavior. Therefore, we call them negative goals (i.e., goals to be avoided); but ambition and pride in achievement are positive goals. Similarly, hopes of winning a parent's love or of reconciliation with a parent are positive goals, which we contrast with fear of estrangement or fear of loss of love. Desires to justify oneself should similarly be contrasted with guilt feelings.

Another distinction that is important has to do with the realistic or unrealistic character of reactive behavior and with its effectiveness in achieving its positive goals. A Demosthenes or a Hannibal compensates for inferiority feelings by a lifelong ambition culminating in supreme achievement, whereas another man's compensation may consist only in idle boasting or in daydreams of being a great man.

Three Kinds of Pride. We often think of pride as satisfaction in being admired by others, which psychoanalysts usually regard as a form of exhibitionism; but pride as a reactive motive probably takes its origin in more elementary urges toward active mastery, which are independent of any concern about being observed. We shall group such reactions together under the concept of "presocial pride."

Presocial Pride. The stimulus for such reactions may be fear, or the memory or fear of helplessness in the face of strong desire, or the threat of an obstacle interfering with a goal-directed striving. The reaction is increased effort in response to an obstacle, or, if the stimulus is fear, there may be a counter-phobic braving of the danger. The essential satisfaction of this kind of pride can be translated into the words "I can." It is a pride in self-assertion, power, or achievement.

A child will often react with a kind of triumphant delight when he first learns to stand or walk or to climb stairs. One child of my acquaintance, when he first succeeded in standing up to hold on to the side of his play pen, remained in this position until he fell asleep. Then he fell back on his pillow. He immediately climbed up again as soon as he woke up, and repeated this performance all day and all night until his parents became alarmed at his loss of sleep. His delight in his achievement was quite independent of any encouragement he received from his parents—since he had received none.

Such reactions to achievement or to the mastery of difficulties can be recognized not only in human beings but in animals as well. They probably are analogous to such physiological reactions as the compensatory hypertrophy of an overloaded heart, or to the development of callous in reaction to irritation of skin or bone. For example, a dog may first run with its tail between its legs when threatened by another dog; but then, detecting some sign of fear in the other dog, will turn and give chase with its tail high in the air! Or a cat will sit motionless, keeping watch over a captured mouse, only to pounce upon it when the mouse gives the least sign of trying to get away. Does the cat derive any satisfaction from thus teasing the mouse? If it were human we would suspect that it is gloating in its power over its helpless prey.

In later life pride in achievement is the motive that most facilitates learning and constructive efforts. On the other hand, in our patients we can observe how the inhibition of aggressive impulses will often give rise to intense feelings of inferiority, because inhibition of aggression makes a person feel weak.

"Exhibitionistic" Pride—Pride in Being Admired or Approved. We must suspect that pride in self-assertion, power, and achievement is based on an inherited mechanism; but other kinds of pride are more or less deliberately inculcated in the child by parents and teachers, by the peer group, and by society at large. Very early, the child develops desires to call attention to himself, to be admired, and to be praised; and feelings of inferiority or shame begin to appear whenever he is seen in an unfavorable light. On account of the fact that society values a number of different kinds of behavior, such socially oriented pride may take any one of a number of different forms.

1. Aggressive efforts to overcome difficulties and to brave danger are important for the survival of the community as a whole. Therefore, the community tends to idealize toughness and boldness and to give honor to the virtues of courage and bravery; and the child's pride in aggressive behavior and achievement tends to be supplemented by pride in exhibiting his prowess or skill to others.

2. On the other hand, the parents and society in general demand compliance from all, and especially from children and women. To this demand the individual may respond by wishes to be approved for being good. On the other hand, the desire to be good may come into conflict with the ambition to be tough; and, consequently, a man may be despised as a weakling if he is too compliant.

3. The criteria for sexual attractiveness are related in somewhat complex ways, which differ for the two sexes, to the two codes of behavior that we have just mentioned. In men, aggressiveness tends to enhance sexual attraction, and being too good or compliant to detract from it. On the other hand, in women, aggressiveness tends to detract from sexual attractiveness except when it can be used provocatively in order to provoke aggression from the male. Moreover, a woman must draw the line with considerable subtlety between being too good and being too seductive.

4. The word "shame" is used in both a general and a more specific sense. As we have already mentioned, Piers (1953) uses the word in its more general sense as equivalent to feelings of inferiority of any kind. In its narrower, more specific sense, it is a *reaction to being seen* by others in an unfavorable light.

Two kinds of experiences are particularly likely to give rise to such feelings of shame (in the narrower sense). One is an experience which almost every child undergoes at some time. At first, the infant is admired for showing himself without clothes to his elders; but then, one day, the elders suddenly hold him up to shame for showing himself in the very way that had previously provoked so much admiration.

Experiences of this kind probably account for the very close association of shame and exhibitionism, to which psychoanalysis has called attention.

The other situation which can activate intense shame is one of betraying erotic feelings toward another person and receiving either no response or a negative response from the object of one's affection.

Such an experience might be compared to taking off one's armour (as an expression of trust and affection) and then discovering that the person to whom one has exposed one's self is really an enemy.

Development of Ego Ideals. We already quoted Freud's concept of the development of the Superego by introjection of parental prohibitions. By a similar process of internalization, the standards according to which a person expects to be judged by the family or by society at large may be incorporated into his own personality and may become an ego ideal by which he judges himself. If then, in the course of time, the standards of society change, or if the individual moves into a new society, he may cling loyally to his own introjected ideals and standards even though they may now conflict with those of the society in which he lives.

Different Kinds of Behavior Inspired by Need for Love. The need for love or fear of loss of love may also result in a number of different kinds of behavior.

Sometimes a person develops patterns based on realistic efforts to win the love of parents and others. The simplest pattern of this kind is one of winning parental approval by being good, by compliance with the consciously expressed moral demands of the parents. Others, during childhood, are not concerned so much with what the parents teach that they should do, but learn rather how to please the parents as persons. Later, such a person may find it very important always to make himself (or herself) pleasing to other people but not necessarily by being good or complying with the demands of society as a whole. In still other cases, a child may become very skillful in adapting to the weaknesses and peculiarities of the parents and others, and in exploiting the weaknesses of others to his own ends, in adroit defiance of the standards of society.

In the past thirty years the psychoanalytic literature has had a great deal to say about the need for punishment, which is usually thought of as a manifestation of a conscious or unconscious sense of guilt. However, such needs for punishment can often be recognized in the child long before there has been introjection of parental prohibitions. The basic mechanism starts with the child's realization or fear that he has offended the parent. To this realization the child then reacts with a hope of reconciliation with the parent by accepting or even provoking punishment. This hope is usually a realistic one, since parents are often willing to accept a child back into their good graces after they have inflicted punishment on him.

Another reaction pattern, which is often confused with a need for punishment and attributed to guilt, is based, I believe, on a much more elementary mechanism. This is the mechanism which I shall call "simple reversal of aggression." By this I mean the mechanism in which an aggressive impulse is turned back against the aggressor in its original form, in which an aggressive impulse is inhibited and then replaced by the fear or wish that someone will do to the aggressor what he originally wished to do to his victim.

A moment ago, we pointed out that a child's hope of reconciliation by means of punishment is a realistic one, based on the actual behavior of parents. But in the mechanism of "simple reversal of aggression" the patient's expectation of being attacked or hurt is not based on any remembered real experience of punishment from a parent. On the contrary, the form of the aggression expected from someone else reproduces the form of the patient's own original aggressive impulse. To account for this reversal we need only assume that *fear of estrangement* from the parent has first caused the original aggressive impulse to be inhibited; and then—because this aggressive impulse must still seek some kind of outlet even after it has been inhibited—it is turned back against the patient himself.

Transition to True Guilt Reactions. The transition from behavior motivated by fear of loss of love to true guilt reactions involves at least two steps.

In the first step, the authority of the parents is replaced in part by acceptance of certain generalized ethical principles that are valid for others as well as for the child himself; and the unconditional desire for the love and approval of parental figures is replaced by a need for self-justification. For example, at a certain stage in ethical development, a child will often use the parent's own words to pass judgment on brothers and sisters, or even on the parents themselves. When an ethical rule has once been accepted by a child it can be thrown into the balance to help justify the child in a controversy between the child and someone else.

But when a child has learned to use an ethical rule to justify himself, the child has not yet developed a conscience. The child can be said to have a conscience only when he has begun to turn the rule back against himself to condemn himself. Then his conscience may stir up in him need for punishment that is independent of the more personal desire to win reconciliation with a parental figure.

Analysis of the Censorship in a Dream. Having now sketched out how reactive motives can be classified, we ask next how one can determine, by analysis of a patient's behavior, what reactive motives have been responsible for his inhibition, repression, or other reaction to a disturbing motive.

One particularly good way to investigate reactive motives is to try to find out what has motivated the censorship in dreams.

In the manifest content of dreams, the latent dream thoughts seem to have undergone distortion. Freud (1900) attributed this distortion to a dream censor. Like a political censor, Freud believed, the dream censor finds certain thoughts unacceptable and excludes them from consciousness. Other thoughts the censor permits to enter consciousness, provided that they first submit to distortion; they are permitted to enter consciousness in disguised form.

Now, in order to study the dreamer's reactive motives, we attempt to analyze the dream censorship:

Let us suppose that we have already discovered the disturbing dream wish. We ask next: Why did this wish have to be censored? What was the "reactive motive" that caused the dream censor to repudiate this particular wish? In order to determine this, we examine the manifest dream and ask how the dreamer has reacted to the disturbing dream wish. For example, if the patient is reacting with feelings of inferiority to an intense dependent wish, in the manifest content we may find him boasting of his independent achievements. If he is reacting with guilt to a hostile impulse the manifest content may picture him as being condemned and submitting to punishment. If the dreamer is reacting with fear of estrangement the manifest content may picture him as seeking reconciliation with a parental figure. The following rather unusually simple example will illustrate how we proceed.

In his first analytic hour, a patient had told of telling both his father and his wife about a current extramarital relationship. The analyst asked why he had done so. In response to this stimulus, the patient that night dreamed as follows:

> "I found myself helpless, unable to use arms and legs and being tortured by two individuals. I promised them that I wouldn't hurt anybody even if I didn't like them. The two individuals seemed to be my father and my brother. I struggled and tried to bite."

Even from the text of this dream it is evident that it is motivated by the patient's need to justify himself. He has reacted to the analyst's question of the preceding hour as though it were an accusation to the effect that his telling his father and his wife were motivated by a desire to hurt them. In the dream text he has pictured a situation in which he would be justified in trying to hurt someone. Being tortured by his father and brother would be ample justification for struggling and trying to bite. Moreover, his promise "that he wouldn't hurt anybody even if he didn't like them" is a protestation of innocence that should still further justify him.

However, the desire to justify himself does not fully account for the manifest dream. The fact that he is unable to use his arms and legs and that, instead of hurting someone, he is being tortured points to an intense reaction formation to his hostile impulses, giving rise first to motor paralysis and then to the turning back of aggression against himself. To account for these two successive reaction formations we must probably postulate guilt as a reactive motive.

Now, putting together these two bits of evidence we can reconstruct the genesis of this dream as follows: The analyst's question stirred up the patient's guilt on account of his desire to hurt both his father and his wife. The dream text implies that he wanted to hurt them not only indirectly by his confession but also by attacking them physically. In the dream work he first reacted to his guilt by a fantasy of paralysis of his arms and legs, and next by one of being tortured. Then, as a second step, he utilized this fantasy of being tortured to justify himself and even to give him an excuse for biting.

BIBLIOGRAPHY

1. Alexander, F. *Roots of Crime*. New York: Alfred A. Knopf, Inc., 1935.
2. ———. "The Relation of Inferiority Feelings to Guilt," *Internat. J. Psychoanal.*, XVIX (1938), 41.
3. French, T. M. "Structural and Functional Approaches to the Analysis of Behavior." In (Grinker, Roy A. (ed.). *Mid-Century Psychiatry*. Springfield, Ill.: Charles S. Thomas, 1953.
4. French, T. M., Alexander, F., *et al. Psychogenic Factors in Bronchial Asthma*. ("Psychosomatic Medicine Monographs," Vol. I,

No. 4; Vol. II, Nos. 1 and 2.) Washington, D. C.: National Research Council, 1941.

5. Freud, A. *Introduction to the Technic of Child Analysis.* New York: Nervous and Mental Disease Publ. Co., 1928.

6. Freud, S. 1900. *The Interpretation of Dreams.* New York: Macmillan Co., 1933.

7. ———. 1914. "On Narcissism—An Introduction." In *Collected Papers,* IV, 30 (3rd ed.). London: Hogarth Press, 1946.

8. ———. 1923. *The Ego and the Id* (4th ed.). London: Hogarth Press, 1947.

9. Piers, G., and Singer, M. *Shame and Guilt.* Springfield, Ill.: Charles C. Thomas, 1953.